First-Rate Reading™ Basics

Comprehension Grades 2-3

by Elizabeth Suarez Aguerre
and Starin W. Lewis

Carson-Dellosa Publishing Company, Inc. • Greensboro, North Carolina

Credits and Dedication

Project Director:

Kelly Gunzenhauser

Editors:

Ellen Gray White, Susan Traylor

Layout Design:

Jon Nawrocik

Inside Illustrations:

Stefano Giorgi

Cover Design:

Peggy Jackson

Cover Illustrations:

Stefano Giorgi

This book is dedicated to my friends and family. Thank you for encouraging me to follow my dreams. Your support has been overwhelming.

-S. L.

Dedicated to Kelly Gunzenhauser,
You have spoiled me for all future editors. Thank you.

-E. S. A.

ISBN 1-59441-045-3

Table of Contents

Introduction

Many reading teachers would argue that all (reading instruction) roads lead to comprehension. Understanding text is the ultimate goal of reading. Phonemic awareness, phonics, fluency, and vocabulary are all important to learn because they assist in comprehension. Without comprehension, reading is a futile pursuit. This book includes many activities to increase comprehension in second and third grades. Some of the activities are literature based, while others are general and can be used with various reading materials.

First-Rate Reading™ *Basics: Comprehension* assumes students have some knowledge of the other four skill sets and takes students beyond basic, word-for-word understanding that is often appropriate for the kindergarten level. Comprehension activities at this level assume that students can read and understand some text for themselves and are capable of searching for meaning through a variety of strategies. Comprehension instruction at this level also assumes that students are ready to make value judgments about the information they read, to determine whether they agree or disagree with it, and also to determine whether they like certain texts and make reading choices based on those likes or dislikes.

Utilize the reproducible Parent Letter (page 5) to help reinforce comprehension instruction at home. The more parents encourage reading and discussion, the more capable their children will be of understanding what they read. The Parent Letter helps inform parents about which skills they impart to their children while reading together and also offers suggestions for making reading experiences even more valuable to young readers.

Finally, use the Assessment (pages 6-7) to look at students' comprehension levels at any time during the school year, including before instruction begins. Giving assessment early will help you determine in which areas students need practice. It will also help you group students by skill level, even if your preference is to group students with a range of skills.

Name _____

Parent Letter

Dear Parents/Family:

Research shows that good readers are more successful in school. Reading is used in all other subjects and is critical for success in real life. It is important for your child to develop a solid reading base that extends beyond phonics into other areas, such as comprehension. Following are suggestions and information about this area of instruction.

Comprehension is the purpose for reading. It allows the reader to make connections between the text and other texts or experiences. Help your child improve comprehension by doing the following:

- Be a good reading role model. Be sure your child sees you reading often.
- Make reading a reward. Use books and reading time as a reward for good behavior, school improvement, etc.
- Take your child to the library to check out books regularly and to attend programs, such as story time, puppet shows, etc.
- Help your child build a home library. An amazing feeling comes with owning books. Create a special bookshelf and let your child earn book money by doing chores or saving allowance.
- Have a weekly or nightly "Family Reading Time." Turn off televisions, computers, and phones, and read. Read a book together, or read independently and share what you are reading about.
- Discuss what your child is reading. Ask "thinking questions," such as, "What do you think will happen next? Why do you think the character did that? How would you feel if you were the character? If you could change anything about the story, what would it be? What's happened so far?"
- Read sections of the newspaper together. Discuss the articles.
- Purchase or borrow books on tape. Have your child listen to a story and follow along with the text.
- Ask your child questions, such as, "What do you like most/least about this story? What do you think will happen next? What is this story about? What happened at the beginning/middle/end?"

Using these ideas will help your child improve reading comprehension. For more information, please feel free to contact me.

Sincerely,

_____

Directions for Comprehension Assessment

Use the following questions for individual assessment. Copy the Comprehension Assessment reproducible (page 7) to record individual student responses. For older or more advanced students, read the questions aloud to small groups and let students write their answers.

1. **Skills: Monitoring comprehension, strategies for self-correction**
   Say, "Pretend that you are reading and come to a word you do not know. List three things you could do to help figure out the meaning of the word."

2. **Skill: Using graphic organizers (This example uses a Venn diagram. If desired, assess students with a different graphic organizer.)**
   Say, "Think about one of your friends. How are you and your friend alike? How are you different? Write some similarities and differences on the diagram." (Have students complete diagrams on separate sheets of paper.)

For the remaining questions, choose a book that is new to students and follow the steps to complete the assessment.

3. **Skill: Pre-reading strategies**
   Show the cover and ask, "What do you think this story will be about? Write your prediction on the lines."

4. **Skills: Generating comprehension questions, pre-reading strategies**
   Say, "Write a question that you want the book to answer."

5. **Skills: Recognizing story structure, answering explicit comprehension questions**
   Read the new book aloud. Ask, "Who are the main characters of the story? Write them next to number 5."

6. **Skills: Recognizing story structure, answering explicit comprehension questions**
   Ask, "What is the book's setting?" or "Where did the story take place?" Have students write their answers.

7. **Skill: Answering implicit comprehension questions**
   Choose a part of the book where a character shows emotion, but the emotion is not directly stated. Show the page and ask, "What do you think the character is feeling here? Why? Write a short answer on the lines."

8. **Skill: Answering scripted comprehension questions**
   Using the same emotion as in question number 7, say, "Write a few sentences about a time that you felt the same way."

9. **Skill: Summarizing**
   Say, "On a separate sheet of paper, write a short summary of the story."

10. **Skill: Responding to text**
    Ask, "What was your favorite part of the story and why? Write your answer on the line."

Comprehension

Follow the directions
your teacher gives you to complete the page.

1. a. _____
   b. _____
   c. _____

2. On a separate sheet of paper, follow your teacher's
   directions to fill in a diagram.

3. _____
   _____

4. _____
   _____

5. _____
   _____

6. _____
   _____

7. _____
   _____

8. _____
   _____

9. On a separate sheet of paper, write a short summary of the story.

10. _____

Pre-Reading Strategies

Introduction

It is critical to teach students strategies they can implement before reading. Many young readers begin reading the first paragraph or page, skipping critical information, such as titles, headings, back cover summaries, cover illustrations, etc. Pre-reading strategies are simple yet extremely effective in aiding comprehension.

Artistic Preview

Help students understand a story better by showing them how to locate specific features before reading a new book. As an example, select a fiction book about birds, such as *Stellaluna* by Janell Cannon (Harcourt, 1993). Before discussing the features of the book, let students make construction paper birdhouses. Give each student a piece of construction paper. Have her fold down the upper left and right corners so that they meet in the middle of the sheet to make a house shape. Have each student draw a circle below the folds and color it black to represent a door. Have her draw a horizontal line below the hole for a perch and draw a bird sitting on the perch. Explain that fiction books usually contain certain features. Write the following fiction text features on the board: *title, cover illustration, text illustration, book jacket, information about the author, information about the illustrator.* Preview the book and have students look for each text feature. Direct students to write each feature under the folds of their birdhouses. Create a display by having students add strips of paper for birdhouse poles. Staple the birdhouses and poles to a bulletin board. Add the title "Birdhouse Preview." To apply this activity to other animal stories, use a dog house for dog stories, a fishbowl for fish stories, etc.

Setting the Purpose

Research has shown that a student's comprehension increases when he reads with a set purpose. Determining a purpose can be done in several ways, depending on the reading material and academic objective. Base the purpose for reading on the reading material. For example, if students are reading a book about pandas, the purpose can be, "Read this book to find out what pandas eat." If students are reading a story about a little girl who travels to another state to visit her grandmother, the purpose might be "Read this story to find out what the little girl learns during her visit with her grandmother." Have students orally set the purpose for each reading selection in a class discussion or with partners. Or, have students write brief sentences beginning with "I will read this to find out . . . ." Tell students to keep their purposes in mind while reading and revisit them after reading.

Nonfiction: Vocabulary Guess

Explain that nonfiction books are books that contain true information about specific subjects. Discuss how nonfiction books usually have some or all of the following features:

- The *table of contents* is a list of the chapters and page numbers.
- The *index* lists the subjects in the book and where they can be found. If readers are looking for a particular subject, they can use the index to go directly to that page.
- A page with *photographs* contains captions next to the photographs that tell the reader what is happening in the pictures.
- *Diagrams* are drawings used to label and show distinct parts.
- There may also be *pronunciation guides* provided in italics after some vocabulary words to show readers how to say words correctly.

After discussing these features, preview a nonfiction book and have students suggest vocabulary words it might contain. For example, words for an insect book could be *thorax, abdomen, antennae, larva,* etc. List the words on chart paper. Assign students to six groups and have each group find the definition of an assigned word in a dictionary or the book's glossary. Ask a student from each group to share the definition of her group's word. Read the book and when you come to a vocabulary word, stop to ask the group to share the definition again. Finally, list the vocabulary words on a word wall or in a class dictionary for students to reference.

Formulating Predictions

Predicting is a simple but powerful reading strategy that helps readers comprehend by giving them something to look for in the text. This strategy correlates to previewing and setting a purpose because predicting cannot occur without previewing, and predictions naturally set a purpose for reading—finding out whether the predictions are correct. Ask students to make simple predictions about what they think a story will be about or add complexity by requiring them to make more specific predictions. For example, if a student is reading a story about a little girl moving to a new neighborhood, he can answer specific prediction questions, such as, "Will the character like her new school? How will the character feel about living next door to her new teacher?" Make sure that students understand that predictions are not about being right; their purpose is to help readers understand what they are reading. Explain that they will learn just as much by comparing what happened to their "wrong" predictions. Young readers' predictions will initially be too simple, so model formulating detailed predictions. For example, if a student says, "I predict that this book will be about a girl and her dog," give a more specific prediction, such as, "I predict that this book will be about a girl who finds a dog, and her parents do not want her to keep it. She tries to convince her parents that she will be responsible enough to care for the dog." Have students read or listen to the text to determine if this prediction is true. Modeling detailed predictions forces students to be more thorough in their previewing and helps them find and identify details in the text. Have students revisit predictions during and after reading to confirm or reject them.

Connecting with Prior Knowledge

Using prior knowledge helps students give logical explanations for what they encounter while using pre-reading strategies. Even if students this young do not understand exactly what a president or prime minister does, they can use what they do know to prepare themselves to read about the offices. Give each student a copy of the Government Leaders reproducible (page 11). Ask, "What do you think is the President's (or Prime Minister's) job? What does he do all day?" Have students write their responses on the reproducible. Continue by asking, "Would you ever like to be the President (Prime Minister) of this country? How do you become President (or Prime Minister) of our country?" Explain that these questions will be answered in a book. Share *So You Want to Be President?* by Judith St. George (Philomel, 2000) or the book and audio recording *Prime Ministers of Canada* by Blaine Selkirk (Sara Jordan, 2001). Identify the answers as they are revealed in the reading. If students are very good readers, provide individual copies of the book for them to read. Have them identify the answers by flagging them with sticky notes, then let them share their answers with the class.

A Visual Comparison

Make students aware that their visual skills are very useful tools to help them learn about text. Select a fiction book with an interesting cover illustration. Stimulate their interest in the book by showing the cover with the title hidden. Then, ask, "What do you think happens in the book?" Have each student write or dictate a short story that could be in the book. Let students share stories with classmates. Read the book aloud and have students compare their stories with the real one. Were any of the stories similar? Finally, discuss with students how writing their own stories and comparing them helped them understand the book better.

Government Leaders

Read the questions.
Write your answers on the lines. In the space below,
draw a picture of yourself as President or Prime Minister.

What is the President's or Prime Minister's job? _____

_____

_____

_____

_____

How do you become the President or Prime Minister?

_____

_____

_____

_____

_____

Journaling with a Purpose

To set a purpose for reading and to access prior knowledge, have students write journal entries about a topic related to the reading material. The journal topic can be very open-ended, such as, "This article is about frogs. Write a paragraph describing the life cycle of a frog." When the journal entries are complete, read a selection that matches the topic of the journal entry you have chosen. Then, have students compare their journal entries with the information contained in the book. Have students complete another journal entry about what they learned from the content read aloud in class. Finally, let students trade entries with classmates. Each student should read the two entries, compare and contrast them, and write a response to the classmate about his entries. For example, a student may read his classmate's entries and write *I see that you live near a pond and see tadpoles swimming in it, so you had a good idea of what they look like before reading the book about the frog's life cycle.*

Webbing for Accessing and Assessing

Graphic organizers, such as webs, can be used with pre-reading activities to access and assess prior knowledge on the reading topic. Webs serve several purposes: students access their prior knowledge before reading about the topic, teachers assess students' existing knowledge and adjust instruction accordingly, and students and teachers revisit webs during and after reading to add newly acquired information and identify misconceptions. For example, if students will read a nonfiction article about the solar system, use the Webbing reproducible (page 13) to assess students' knowledge prior to reading. After reading, have students revisit their webs to highlight correct information and cross out incorrect information. Have them use different-colored pens to add information that was gained by reading. Webs can also be used with fictional reading material by having students brainstorm information about the theme. For example, if students will read a novel that takes place on a farm, have them web everything they know about farm animals prior to reading the book. Have students use the Webbing reproducible to access prior knowledge, then revisit the reproducible after they have read the book.

Webbing

Write a topic in the center oval.
In the other ovals, write facts about the topic.

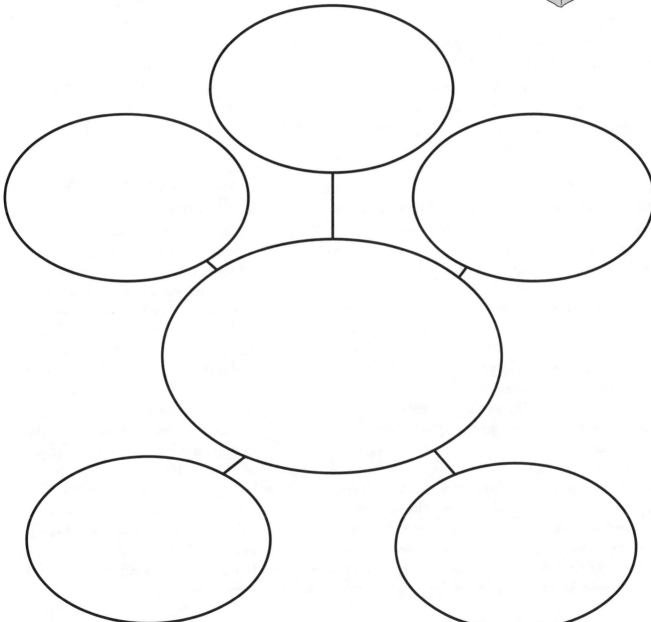

Monitoring Comprehension

Introduction

As students become better readers, their ability to improve comprehension through monitoring should improve. Students in second and third grades should be less focused on decoding and more focused on understanding the big picture of their reading. Additionally, students should attempt to read more books independently, which gives them more opportunities to check their understanding than having books read to them. Use these strategies to push students toward a more independent way of reading and understanding.

Skimming and Scanning

This basic reading strategy is not natural to young readers and should be explicitly taught. Tell students that good readers do not always read every single word. Sometimes readers have to look quickly at the text (skim or scan) to look for information. Have students suggest possible scenarios in which skimming/scanning would be useful, such as looking for particular words, previewing text, looking for answers to questions, finding the last place that was read when picking up a book again, etc. Demonstrate skimming by copying a passage onto a transparency and using your finger or a bookmark to quickly move along text while looking for a particular word or phrase. Have students practice this strategy with the following activity. Assign students to teams. Using the same reading material for everyone, such as a reading textbook or other textbook, a supplemental article, etc., challenge the teams to skim/scan the text to find a particular word or phrase. The first team to find the word or phrase must raise their hands and explain where in the text the word or phrase is found. Give points to teams who skim and find the word or phrase the quickest. For a variation on this game, have student pairs challenge each other to skim text and find selected words or phrases.

Selective Highlighting and Underlining

Explain that one way to monitor comprehension and track important information is to highlight or underline words or phrases. Use an overhead projector and a copy of an informational article to model how to highlight and underline important information encountered while reading. Explain that this is called selective because students will select only very important information to highlight or underline. Have students practice this strategy on informational text, newspaper articles, etc. This strategy is also useful with narrative text to identify critical vocabulary, important scenes, etc. Be sure students know not to use this strategy in borrowed library books or textbooks. Instead, introduce students to using sticky notes for this purpose.

Problems and Solutions

Explain that good readers know when they do not understand what they are reading. Instead of ignoring the problem, good readers stop and try to fix the problem. Ask, "If you do not understand what you are reading, what can you do?" Write students' suggestions on a piece of chart paper. Include the following strategies.

- Go back and reread the sentence.
- Use the context of the words.
- Use the pictures to figure out the meaning.
- Sound out a difficult word.*
- Look back in the story. (Maybe something was mentioned earlier that will help you understand.)
- Glance forward in the story. (Look at chapter titles and illustrations to see if the answer is coming up.)

Post the list in the classroom. Add new strategies as students learn them. Occasionally stop during reading time to demonstrate how to use one or two of the strategies so that students are reminded to do the same in their own independent reading.

*Sounding out a difficult word is included in the list of comprehension strategies even though it is considered a phonics strategy. The ability to decode puzzling words is a skill that strengthens students' comprehension skills.

Signal Flags

On a piece of white construction paper, draw a red X from corner to corner to make a flag. Tell students that this is the "teacher's flag," and it means "I need help." Help students create flags similar to International Maritime Signal Flags that mean, "I have something to tell you." For every two students, cut a piece of black construction paper in half twice to create four black squares. Give each student a whole piece of yellow construction paper and two black squares. Have each student turn the yellow paper horizontally and glue one black square to the top right side of the yellow paper and the other black square to the lower left section. Have each student write strategies from the Problems and Solutions activity (above) on the yellow parts of her flag. Then, read a story aloud, occasionally "getting stuck." Think aloud to show students how to know when they have made mistakes. For example, say, "I just said that the boy lived in a *horse*. That does not make any sense. A boy cannot live in a *horse*. I must have made a mistake." When you make a mistake, wave your flag to ask for help. Explain that when you wave your flag, students should suggest strategies to fix the problem. When a student has a strategy to share, she should wave her black and yellow flag to signal, "I have something to tell you!" Use the student's strategy to correct your mistake.

"Monitor"-ing Comprehension

When students have trouble understanding a story, give them some "key" ideas to solve the problem. Give each student a copy of the "Monitor"-ing Comprehension reproducible (page 17). Explain that the computer monitor will help students remember to monitor their comprehension. Have students read the following sentences on the monitor section of the reproducible: *While reading, monitor what you do understand. Stop when you do not understand something.* Have students read the following "key" concepts on the keyboard section of the reproducible to help them understand what they are reading.

- Go back and reread the sentence.
- Use the pictures.
- Use the meaning (context) of the words.
- Sound out a hard word.
- Look back in the story to find clues.
- Glance ahead to see if future pages will answer questions.

Have each student cut out his computer and fold it on the line between the monitor and keyboard so that the reproducible looks like a computer monitor with a keyboard in front of it. Allow students to keep their computers at their desks for reference.

Buddy Brains

This quick, simple strategy helps students monitor their own comprehension while reading actively in either whole group or independent readings. This strategy supports struggling readers by giving them opportunities to connect with the reading and with partners. Tell students that two brains are better than one and that they will be using their buddies' brains throughout the reading. Assign nearby reading buddies. During pre-reading activities, have each student quickly share his predictions with a buddy. As each student reads the text, have him periodically discuss or share thoughts with his buddy. For example, if students are reading an article about protecting the environment that states that there are many things people can do to conserve water, have each student share one way to save water at home. The key to this strategy is to reinforce meaning by having each student turn to a buddy repeatedly to quickly respond to the reading, interact with the buddy, or answer a question about the reading.

Active Reading

Students' comprehension increases dramatically when students read actively and focus on content. Use the Active Reading reproducibles (pages 18-19) to engage students in active reading. Active reading charts give students opportunities to answer their questions, make predictions about events, record information learned, or respond to text in a specific manner. Model how to complete the charts prior to instructing students to do so independently. As students become more proficient in using each comprehension strategy, they will also become more proficient readers.

First-Rate Reading™: Comprehension • CD-104015 • © Carson-Dellosa
Basics

"Monitor"-ing Comprehension

Read the "key" ways you can
fix your comprehension if you are having problems. Cut out the picture
and fold on the line between the computer and keyboard.

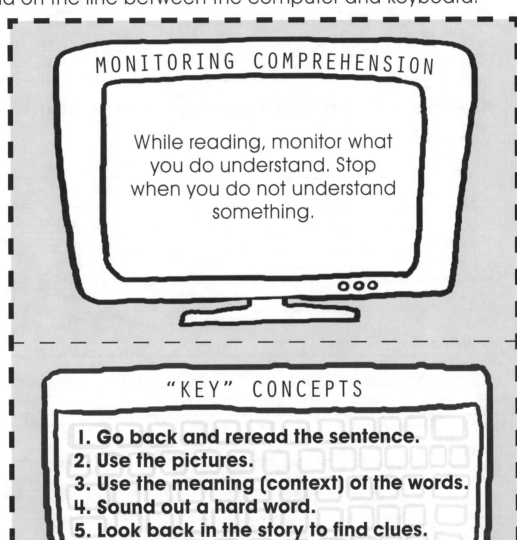

MONITORING COMPREHENSION

While reading, monitor what you do understand. Stop when you do not understand something.

"KEY" CONCEPTS

1. Go back and reread the sentence.
2. Use the pictures.
3. Use the meaning (context) of the words.
4. Sound out a hard word.
5. Look back in the story to find clues.
6. Glance ahead to see if future pages will answer questions.

Active Reading Chart: Informational

In the spaces below, write new
words and important facts you learned while reading.
Use the information you record to help you understand and remember
what you read. Use more pages if necessary.

Book Title: _____

New vocabulary and definitions found in the text:

Vocabulary word: _____

Definition: _____

_____

Vocabulary word: _____

Definition: _____

_____

Vocabulary word: _____

Definition: _____

_____

Vocabulary word: _____

Definition: _____

_____

Important facts I've read:

_____

_____

_____

_____

First-Rate Reading™ Comprehension • CD-104015 • © Carson-Dellosa
Basics

Active Reading Chart: Narrative

In the spaces below, write about characters you have met and problems that have happened in the story. Then, make predictions for what will happen. Use the information you record to help you understand and remember what you read. Use more pages if necessary.

Book Title: _____

Characters

Character #1: _____

Character #2: _____

Character #3: _____

Character #4: _____

Problems

Problem #1: _____

_____

Problem #2: _____

_____

Problem #3: _____

_____

Predictions

_____

_____

_____

_____

Comprehension with Visualization

Young readers need to learn how to visualize what they read in order to better understand text and monitor their own comprehension. A concrete way to help students learn this strategy is to tell them that they should see the action happening in the reading in their minds as if there are television screens in their minds. Compare a "Brain TV" to a computer or television screen. When first teaching this powerful strategy, have students close their eyes and "see" or visualize on their Brain TVs what you describe. Describe a very detailed, simple scene, such as, "The sun burned brightly in the clear blue sky. The ocean's waves splashed on the shore. The little girl ran quickly toward the water as the hot sand burned her bare feet." Then, have several students describe what they "saw" in their heads. Ask, "How did you picture the little girl? Did she look like someone you know? What color was her swimsuit? Did you see her facial expression as she ran?" Then, describe the same scene with even greater detail and have students visualize again. For example, say "The sun burned brightly in the cloudless, pale blue sky. The cool ocean water splashed loudly on the shore. The beach was packed with families swimming playfully in the water, children building sand castles, and people having picnic lunches on blankets. The little girl with the pink ruffled swimsuit ran quickly toward the water as the hot sand burned her bare feet. Her face was crumpled as she shrieked with each step." Discuss how the visualizing of each scene was different. Use the Turn on Your "Brain TV" reproducible (page 21) to practice visualization techniques. Select a descriptive scene from a book or story. Look for one in which there are many details and a lot of action. Then, read the scene and instruct students to picture everything on their Brain TVs. Have each student draw what she "saw" on the TV screen. Let students compare drawings and revisit the text, finding the words and phrases that helped them visualize the scene.

Bookmark Solutions

When a student does not understand something and continues to read, he may miss key information in the text. Help students make useful bookmarks that will provide reminders of strategies to monitor their comprehension. Explain that it is important for students to recognize when they do not understand what they read and to know how to do something about it. Give each student a bookmark from the Comprehension Bookmarks reproducible (page 22). Allow students to decorate the backs of bookmarks. (Punch holes in the tops and tie yarn tassels to them, if desired.) Review various comprehension strategies for students to use, such as rereading the text, using pictures for clues, trying to sound out a word, looking back to see if they missed things, and looking ahead to see if their questions are answered in the next few pages or chapters. Explain that students should understand various strategies because one strategy will not work in all situations. Allow time for students to read independently. Give students a few small sticky notes to place on pages where they do not understand the text. Have them try a few of the strategies from the bookmarks. Then, work with students in small groups. Have them describe their difficulties, which strategies they tried, and what worked.

Turn on Your "Brain TO"

Choose a scene from the reading
to draw on the TV below. Include as much detail as you can.

Comprehension Bookmarks

Copy and cut out bookmarks for students.

Know what you understand and what you do not understand. If you do not understand what you are reading, try one of these strategies:

1. Reread the text.

2. Use the pictures for clues.

3. Sound out a difficult word.

4. Use the context of the words.

5. Look back in the story to see if you missed something.

6. Look forward in the story to see if your question is answered in the next few pages.

Know what you understand and what you do not understand. If you do not understand what you are reading, try one of these strategies:

1. Reread the text.

2. Use the pictures for clues.

3. Sound out a difficult word.

4. Use the context of the words.

5. Look back in the story to see if you missed something.

6. Look forward in the story to see if your question is answered in the next few pages.

Comprehension Bag of Tricks

Students need to learn that even good readers sometimes have trouble while reading. Give examples of situations in which a proficient reader might "get stuck," such as reading unfamiliar material, reading material that is low-interest or pertaining to a subject that the reader is not familiar with, encountering new words, etc. Discuss what a reader might do when he "gets stuck" while reading, such as ask someone else for help, consult a dictionary, think about what the story is about, reread, replace an unfamiliar word with a word that would make sense in context, read on and then return to the unfamiliar word to see if he can figure out what it is, ask himself what makes sense, pause after each paragraph or page to summarize what he's read so far, etc. The list is endless and can be added to throughout the year. Tell students that these techniques are like tricks to fix their reading problems, much like a magician has a "bag of tricks." Let students use enlarged copies of the Comprehension Tricks reproducible (page 24) to compile lists of possible solutions to reading problems. Have students keep their bags at their desks for reference and add to them as they learn new techniques.

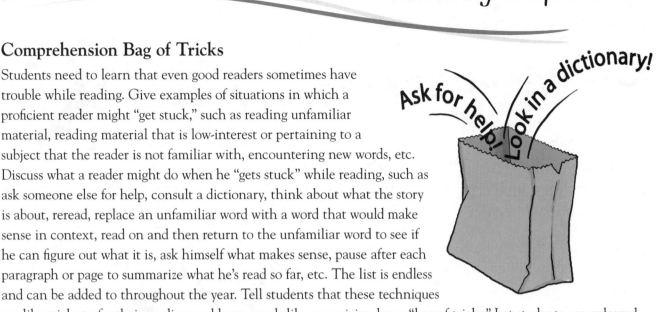

A Condensed Version

One way for students to monitor their own comprehension is to retell stories in their own words. As students retell, you and they will know if they understand them. Have students write condensed versions of the story *The Stinky Cheese Man and Other Fairly Stupid Tales* by Jon Scieszka (Viking, 1992). Tell students that a condensed version is a shorter version of a story that contains main plot elements but leaves out some descriptions and perhaps some secondary plot material. Cut pieces of white paper into fourths measuring 4 1/4" x 5 1/2" (10.8 cm x 14 cm) to make mini-pages. Give each student five mini-pages. Have students staple the pages together along the left sides to make mini-books. On the fronts, direct students to decorate the covers and write the title "The Condensed Version of *The Stinky Cheese Man*." After you read each story in the book, stop and have each student write his retelling of the first story on the first mini-page. Remind students to be aware of whether they comprehend the story by thinking about how confident they feel about retelling it. Continue reading and have students write their versions of each story. Have students write on the fronts and backs of the pages. Ask, "What are some things you can do if you do not understand what you are reading?" Explain that students need to be able to retell stories that they read independently. If they cannot, they should try strategies to help them understand the stories better.

Comprehension Tricks

Just like magicians, good
readers have "bags of tricks" they can use to fix
their reading problems. On the bag of tricks, write some of the
strategies you like to use to help you understand what you are reading.

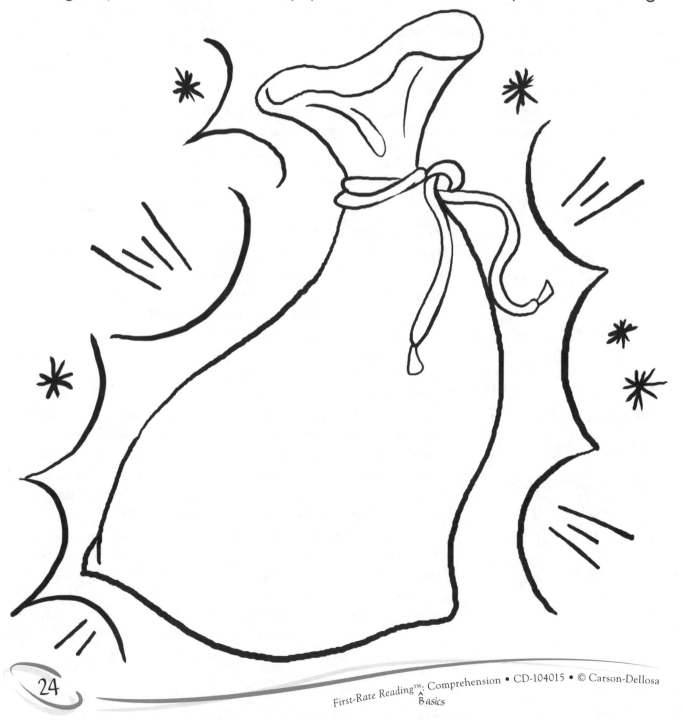

Graphic and Semantic Organizers

Introduction

Graphic organizers (webs, charts, graphs, maps, and diagrams) provide a visual framework that helps students interpret, organize, and represent relationships found in text. Graphic organizers can be used prior to reading to access prior knowledge, make predictions, and set a purpose for reading. They can be used during reading fiction or nonfiction to engage students in active reading and help them monitor what they read and focus on the text. Or, they can be used after reading to organize, categorize, and summarize information. Semantic organizers connect related ideas, events, and concepts. Second- and third-grade students should be able to use organizers with ease.

KWL Chart

Using a KWL chart helps students classify what they know, what they would like to find out, and what they learned from their reading. Preview a book with students, then copy the KWL Chart reproducible (page 26) onto a transparency. Ask students what information they know from their preview. Maybe they know that the book will address the water cycle since the title of the book is *The Life of a Raindrop*. After filling in the K (know) column, ask students what they want to know and fill in the W (want to know) column. Use this space to ask questions students would like answered. Finally, after you read the book, fill in the L (learned) column with information students learned while reading, especially if the information answers some of the questions. When students are familiar with this format, allow them to use the reproducible with their own reading. Collect the sheets to assess comprehension.

SWBST

SWBST stands for Somebody Wanted But So Then. Explain that in fiction, a plot is often driven by characters who want different things. Demonstrate by having students choose to reread a short, favorite book with a strong protagonist, such as *Lilly's Purple Plastic Purse* by Kevin Henkes (Greenwillow, 1996). Pair students and give each pair a copy of the SWBST reproducible (page 27). Read the book with students. Then, assign each pair a character. Even though different pairs have different characters, fill in the reproducibles as a class. Start by saying, "In the blank next to the word *Somebody*, write the name of the character you were assigned." Then, have students fill in what they think their characters *Wanted* at particular points in the book. For example, at the beginning of the book, Lilly wanted to show off her new purse, and Mr. Slinger wanted to teach his class. Tell students that what characters want can change throughout the book, but there is often a main desire that each character has. Next, have students decide what is getting in the way of what the characters want. For example, Lilly wants to show off her purse, *But* Mr. Slinger asks her not to and takes it away. Use the *So, then* portion to show how the problems are resolved. Then, let students suggest how to fill in the main idea portion. Let students use additional copies of the reproducible to do independent character analysis.

KWL Chart

Before reading, fill in the K column
on the chart below. Try to include everything you think you know about
the topic or story. Fill in the W column with things you want to know
about the topic or story. Keep this chart in mind while you read. Then,
fill in the L column to show what you learned.

Topic or story title: _____

K	W	L
(know)	(want to know)	(learned)
_____	_____	_____
_____	_____	_____
_____	_____	_____
_____	_____	_____
_____	_____	_____
_____	_____	_____
_____	_____	_____
_____	_____	_____

Look at your chart. Did you find out that any of your K information was
incorrect? If so, what? _____

_____

Did the reading answer all of your W questions? If not, where do you
think you can find these answers? _____

_____

Name ______________________________

SWBST

Fill in the chart below.
After completing the chart,
write the main idea on the lines provided.

Topic or story title: ______________________________

Somebody (character/s): ______________________________

____

Wanted (goal): ______________________________

____

But (problem): ______________________________

____

So, then (solution): ______________________________

____

Main Idea: ______________________________

____

____

____

Main Idea Treasure

As students move from picture books to chapter books and from simple informational text to more complex reading, it will become more difficult for them to easily state the main idea in their reading. Help students practice this skill with the Main Idea Treasure reproducible (page 29). Explain that sometimes, the main idea is like a hidden treasure. Just like there are often clues to a hidden treasure, an author often gives clues to a main idea but does not state exactly what it is. Give each student a copy of the reproducible and an article in which the main idea is not obviously stated. Have students read the article. Then, have them write clues the author gives and what they think the main idea is. Collect the papers and assess students' grasp of reading for main idea. Repeat the activity with a fiction chapter book. Allow each student to prepare one copy of the reproducible for a chapter and a second copy for the entire book. Again, assess students' understanding. When students can find the main idea with more difficult material, pair students with partners who have the same reading material and let them assess each other's work, or have them work together to find the main idea.

Supporting Details

Revisit the concept of main idea by having students think about it from another perspective. Ask, "What would happen if you broke a leg from a table? The table would probably fall. That is because the legs support the table. A main idea is like that, too. The main idea is supported by details. Without supporting details, a main idea would 'fall,' too." Choose a familiar picture book or short chapter book students have already read as an example, or use a reading selection from the Main Idea Treasure activity (above). Let students use the Supporting Details reproducible (page 30) to write the main idea and its supporting details. Have students explain how they knew what the main idea was. Lead a discussion about how, without the supporting details, students would not know what the main idea is. Then, choose another familiar book and have students reread it and complete other copies of the reproducible for practice.

Problems and Solutions

Similar to the SWBST activity (page 25), this activity helps students see complicated issues in simple terms. Review that most stories have problems that need solutions. In fact, having a problem to solve indicates to students that they are reading a narrative story, rather than a descriptive, persuasive, or informational piece (although these can overlap). Have students read a chapter book, such as *Frog and Toad Together* by Arnold Lobel (HarperCollins, 1972), then assign students to small groups. Make each group responsible for a different chapter. Give each group a copy of the Problems and Solutions reproducible (page 31) and have them write the problems in the chapter along with their solutions. (For *Frog and Toad Together*, there are only a few problems, so it is a good book to use for practice.) For example, for the chapter "The Garden," students may write that the problem is that Toad wants to grow a garden, and the solution is for Toad to be patient. Let each group discuss their problems and solutions, and allow other groups to add more. Finally, read a chapter from another *Frog and Toad* book, and let students complete Problem and Solution reproducibles independently.

Main Idea Treasure

On the treasure map below,
write clues the author gives about what
the main idea might be. When you think you know it, write the main
idea on the treasure chest.

Clues

Main Idea

Name _____

Supporting Details

Write a supporting detail from
your reading on each table leg. Write the main idea on the tabletop.

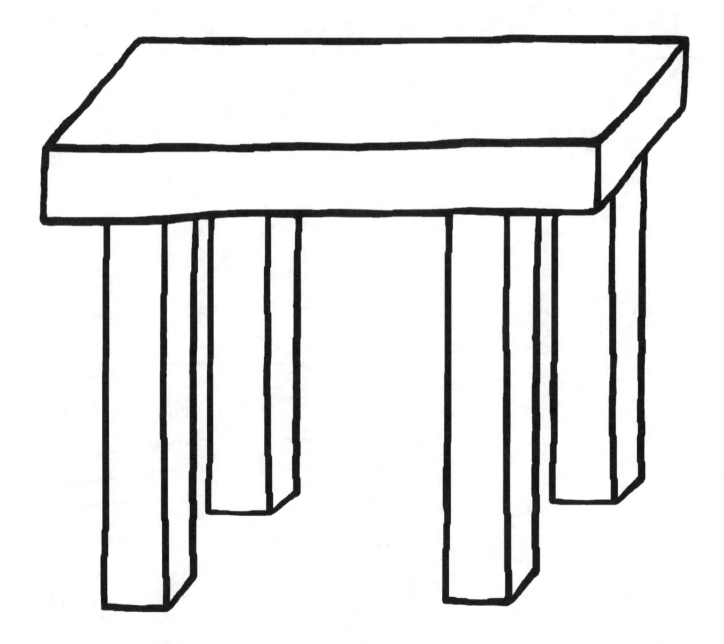

First-Rate Reading™: Comprehension • CD-104015 • © Carson-Dellosa
Basics

Problems and Solutions

List the problems in the story in the
first column. Write how each problem is solved in the second column.

Problems	Solutions

Prove It!

Even though much of students' work with books and text will center around finding facts, remind them that their opinions are valuable, too. Ask each student to think of a book she feels strongly about, either positively or negatively. Have students spend a few minutes explaining to partners why they have the strong feelings. Next, allow students to independently fill out copies of the Prove It! reproducible (page 33). Schedule time for students to present their opinions. If two students choose the same book, have those students present on the same day. As students present, keep copies of their books nearby to check how their opinions are related to actual facts in the books. For example, if a student says that she likes *Charlotte's Web* by E. B. White (HarperTrophy, 1974) because the characters are nice, then she may only have skimmed the book. But, if a student says that he likes the book because he loves reading about how Templeton gorges himself at the fair, then he has probably read more carefully. Collect students' papers and assist those who seem to need more guidance.

Cause and Effect

Students can see patterns in text when they study cause and effect. It helps them to know that actions and reactions are not random. Understanding how a character has reacted in the past will help students predict how she may act in the future. Cause and effect also helps students sequence events. Assign a book to read that has definite causes and effects, such as *Martha Speaks* by Susan Meddaugh (Houghton Mifflin, 1992). Group students and give each group a copy of the Cause and Effect reproducible (page 34). When students have read the book, state a cause from the book for students to copy on the reproducibles. Let groups come up with the effect. For example, say, "Martha ate a bowl of alphabet soup." Students should write that in the *Causes* column, then write *Martha learned to talk* in the *Effects* column. Next, give an effect, such as, "Police officers caught the burglars." Students should write that in the *Effects* column, then write *Martha ate more soup and called the police* in the *Causes* column. Have students use additional copies of the reproducible for other books. Students can also use this reproducible effectively with some nonfiction.

Making Connections

Using a Venn diagram can help students see connections between books. Since many students have used Venn diagrams frequently by second or third grade, use a more sophisticated version that asks additional comprehension questions. Use two books from a series, such as *Miss Nelson Is Missing!* (Houghton Mifflin, 1977) and *Miss Nelson Is Back* (Houghton Mifflin, 1982) by Harry Allard. Give each student a copy of the Making Connections reproducible (page 35) on which to compare the two books. Tell students to write the title of the first book in the first oval and the title of the second book in the second oval. While you read both books, tell students to think about what is the same in the two books and what is different. For example, Miss Nelson is absent in both books, and her students miss her. But in *Miss Nelson Is Missing!*, the students get a horrible substitute teacher, whereas in *Miss Nelson Is Back*, they are taught by the principal. Work with students to compare and contrast the two stories using the diagram. Let students use additional copies of the reproducible to work on comparing other books.

Prove It!

Write your opinions in the column
on the left. Find proof from the reading to support your opinions. Write
proof from the reading in the column on the right.

My Opinions	Proof from the Text to Support My Opinions

Cause and Effect

Use the graphic organizer
to list the causes and their effects.

Causes	→	Effects
_____		_____
_____		_____
_____		_____
_____		_____
_____		_____
_____		_____
_____		_____
_____		_____

Pick a cause and effect from the graphic organizer. Fill in the blanks
below to write a sentence.

_____
(effect)

because _____ .
(cause)

First-Rate Reading™: Comprehension • CD-104015 • © Carson-Dellosa
Basics

Making Connections

Write the first book title
in the first oval. Write the second book title
in the second oval. Write things that are different about the books
in the ovals. Write things that are the same in the part that overlaps.
Then, complete the paragraph at the bottom of the page.

differences   similarities   differences

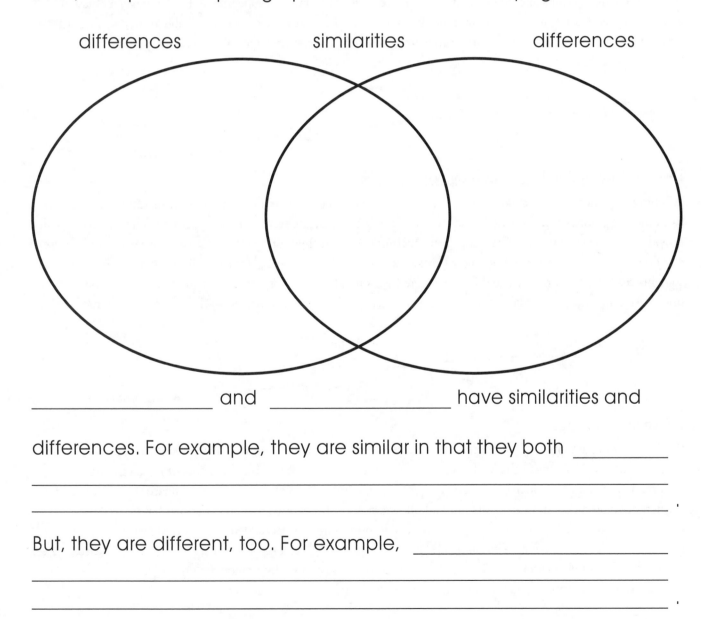

_____ and _____ have similarities and

differences. For example, they are similar in that they both _____

_____

_____ .

But, they are different, too. For example, _____

_____

_____ .

Character Analysis

Readers learn a lot about stories and improve their comprehension by learning how to analyze characters. Authors use many different techniques to help the reader "get to know" characters: telling characters' actions, using dialogue, describing appearances, etc. Help students improve their inferring, critical thinking, recognition of patterns in narrative text, etc., through character analysis. Let students use the Character Analysis reproducible (page 37) to analyze a character. Have students find examples of each category (actions, appearance, and dialogue) in the text and write them in the appropriate sections of the web. After students complete the web, ask, "Does the author choose to use more dialogue to let the reader know what the character is like? Or, does the author use action to provide insight about the character? How important is the character to the story?" Help students identify that a character's actions and dialogue often tell more about her than her appearance. For example, a character who cries quietly in her room, walks with her head down, and avoids eye contact is probably unhappy, shy, or afraid. Have students use the Prove It! reproducible (page 33) to support their opinions about a character with proof from the text.

Pre- and Post-Reading Webbing

Webbing activities are particularly useful with nonfiction text but can be used with any genre. Give each student two different-colored pens or pencils and a copy of the Web Organizer reproducible (page 38). The two colors will provide an easy visual for students to see how much information they can learn from text. Have each student use one pen to web everything she knows (or thinks she knows) about a topic prior to reading about it. Then, have students read the text and use the different-colored pens to add new information and cross out any erroneous information on their webs. Have students compare their pre-reading information to their post-reading information.

Partner Webbing

Partner webbing activities help students see the value of cooperative work. Give each student two different-colored pens or pencils and a copy of the Web Organizer reproducible (page 38). Have each student read a passage and use one pen to complete a web on the text's topic. Then, pair students and have them compare their webs. Using a different-colored pen, have each student add information to the webs that his partner had but he did not. Have students compare the information they wrote to the information that was added after working with partners. Discuss the value of cooperative grouping and how each student is responsible for learning from what he reads and should share this information with his partner. Extend the activity by adding more colors and more partners to see how much more information can be obtained when several people work together.

First-Rate Reading™: Comprehension • CD-104015 • © Carson-Dellosa
Basics

Name _____

Character Analysis

Fill in information on this web
about a character in a book you have read.

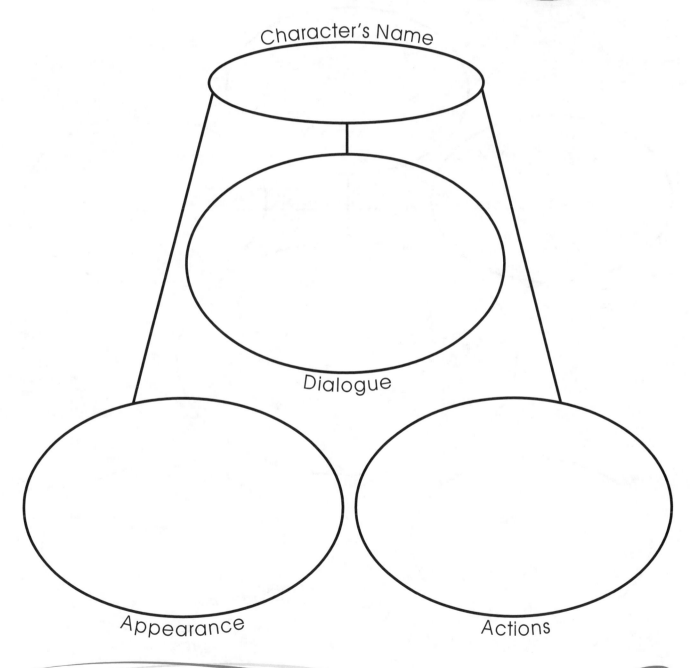

Character's Name

Dialogue

Appearance

Actions

Name _____

Web Organizer

Use this graphic organizer
to help you categorize information from
your reading. Add more sections if needed.

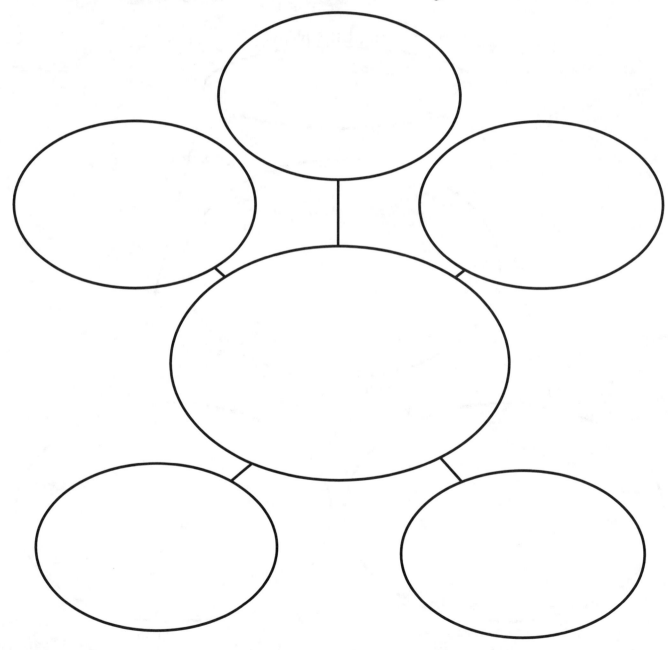

First-Rate Reading™: Comprehension • CD-104015 • © Carson-Dellosa
Basics

Answering and Generating Comprehension Questions

Introduction

Having students answer comprehension questions is a tried-and-true teaching technique. If students know the questions before they read, they find a purpose for reading and a reason to personally connect to the text. Students benefit from being able to identify different types of questions because they will know where and how to look for the answers.

Two basic categories of comprehension questions are *lower-order* and *higher-order*. Lower-order questions are factual, with answers that can be found directly in the text. Higher-order questions involve critical thinking. In other words, students must form their own opinions and then connect them to what is in the text in order to answer. Young students usually find these two categories sufficient. Older or more advanced students may benefit from dividing lower-order and higher-order into additional subcategories as stated in the QAR method of questioning originated by Taffy Raphael in the 1980s (Raphael, T. E. (1986). Teaching Question Answer Relationships, revisited. *The Reading Teacher* 39 (6):516-522.) Lower-order question subcategories can be *explicit* (right there) or *implicit* (think and search). Answers to explicit questions can be underlined in the text. Answers to implicit questions can be found in the text, but a student must be able to integrate sections or the entire book to find them. Below are examples of explicit and implicit questions from *Charlotte's Web* by E. B. White (HarperTrophy, 1974).
- Explicit question: How many goslings hatched? (seven)
- Implicit question: What did Charlotte do to keep Wilbur from being butchered? (She wrote slogans about him in her webs that made him famous.)

Higher-order questions can be further divided into *inductive* (author and reader) and *scriptal* (on your own). Inductive (author and reader) questions involve using the text to determine the author's implied meaning or intention; the answers are more complex than facts found in the text. Scriptal questions may require students to use their knowledge of the text as a backdrop, but they do not have to refer directly to anything in the text. Below are examples of inductive and scriptal questions from *Charlotte's Web*.
- Inductive question: Why did Charlotte decide to save Wilbur? (She saved Wilbur because she was kind and clever. She also liked Wilbur and wanted him to live a long life, even if she could not. Student answers will vary but are correct as long as they can be substantiated in the text.)
- Scriptal question: What would you have done to save Wilbur? (Answers will vary.)

After students have learned how to classify questions, teach them to generate questions. When students write comprehension questions, they have to think of the answers. This helps students grasp concepts in the text. Generating questions also encourages students to look for information throughout the text. When a question comes from you, students may focus on one part of the story, but when students have to write the questions, they look through the entire text to come up with ideas.

Comparing Questions

Guide students to find patterns in the wording of lower-order and higher-order questions. Students will discover that many higher-order questions start with *how, why, what do you think, why do you think that, what would you do if, what might have made the character, if you,* etc. Many lower-order questions begin with one of the basic "question words" (*what, when, who, where*). Write a selection of text-related questions and have students work in pairs to answer the questions and identify them as lower-order or higher-order. Tell students to be prepared to defend their identifications of lower-order or higher-order. Compare answers, then have students further categorize the questions as *explicit, implicit, inductive,* or *scriptal.* Give students copies of the Question Types Reference reproducible (page 41) to use during the activity.

Sorting Questions

Write several text-based questions on index cards (one per card). Prepare equal numbers of lower- and higher-order questions. Shuffle the cards and assign students to small groups. Give an equal number of cards to each group and instruct groups to keep the cards facedown until you say, "Go." Then, have the groups compete against each other to quickly sort their question cards into lower-order and higher-order stacks. The first group to correctly sort all of their cards earns a point. Have other groups continue sorting, then have groups reshuffle cards and exchange stacks. Continue until all groups have seen all of the cards or until a group earns a predetermined point total.

Creating Who, What, When, and Where Questions

Students benefit from creating their own comprehension questions. When they understand the thinking process required to create a question, they are better able to go through the thinking process required to answer one. Use the think-aloud method to model how to write a lower-order question using familiar text. Think aloud as you create the question so that students can "see" the thinking process and steps required for the activity. For example, say, "I'm going to write a lower-order question. I know that lower-order questions are pretty easy to answer because they only require the person answering to reread the text to find the answer. I also know that these questions often start with words such as *what, who, when,* or *where.* As I skim the story, I find a section with some good information for a question. *Abby put on her favorite sweater for the first day of school. It was a very colorful sweater—like a rainbow.* I can write a lower-order question starting with the word *what. What was Abby's sweater like?* It says right here in the text that Abby's sweater was *like a rainbow.*" Have students work in small groups to generate lower-order questions. Then, have groups take turns posing their questions to the rest of the class and challenging other groups to find the answers as quickly as possible.

First-Rate Reading™: Comprehension • CD-104015 • © Carson-Dellosa
Basics

Name _____

Question Types Reference

Use this page to help
you remember differences between
lower-order and higher-order questions.

Lower-order questions use low brain power, are easy to answer, have answers that are right in the text, and often start with *What, When, Who,* or *Where.*

Examples:
What material did the first little pig use to build his house?
Who was trying to blow the houses down?
Where did the first and second little pigs hide?

Higher-order questions use high brain power, are harder to answer, have answers that are not right in the text, require you to think of the answers with your brain, and often start with *How, Why, What would you do,* or *If you.*

Examples:
How did the first little pig feel when the wolf came to his door?
Why do you think the wolf wanted to eat the little pigs?
If you were the third little pig, would you let your brothers in your house?

Lower-order questions	Higher-order questions
Explicit/right-there questions • have short answers • have answers that are listed in the text	**Inductive/author-and-you questions** • require you to think about what the author meant • have answers that are not found right in the text
Implicit/think-and-search questions • have answers that you must look through several pages to find	**Scriptal/on-your-own questions** • require you to think about your opinions and experiences to answer them

Just the Facts

Explain that when reporters ask questions that start with the words *who, what, when,* and *where,* they are looking for facts. Reporters also ask questions that start with the word *did.* As an example, have students be reporters covering a story about a hero fish named Big Al. Afterwards, have them answer questions that are answered in the book. Read the story *Big Al* by Andrew Clements (Aladdin, 1988). Give each student a copy of the Just the (Fish) Facts reproducible (page 43). Remind students that the questions are lower-order questions; the author has written the answers to these questions in the book. Review each question and allow students to look back through the book if needed. When the "reporters" are finished, review the answers (below).

Answers may vary:

1. The story occurred in the ocean.
2. Big Al was a very nice fish who looked scary.
3. Big Al tried to blend in, hide his size, and crack jokes.
4. Yes. Big Al broke through the net.
5. Big Al freed the other fish.

Creating and Answering Higher-Order Questions

Higher-order questions will be challenging for students to create and may require more practice than lower-order questions. Select a story that students have read and discussed. Use the prompts on the Question Creators reproducible (page 44) to help students generate questions about different text elements, such as main event, cause and effect, etc. Make several enlarged copies of the reproducible, cut apart the question creator cards, and laminate them. Pair students and give each pair a question creator card. Consider pairing struggling students with students who understand how to create comprehension questions or repeat the think-aloud process described in Creating Who, What, When, and Where Questions (page 40). The question creator cards will cue students to begin thinking about what types of questions require the reader to utilize information provided by the author and will help them integrate this knowledge with previously learned information to provide original answers. Have each pair write a question about the story on a sheet of paper using their card as a guide. They should write in their answer on the back of the paper. Remind students that for higher-order questions, answers will vary. Have pairs exchange questions and answer them. Then, have students share their questions and answers and decide as a class if the questions they created required higher-order thinking. For additional practice with narrative or informational text, have students complete and answer questions from the Higher-Order Question Starters reproducible (page 45). For more traditional practice questions that students do not have to complete first, have students answer items from the Higher-Order Comprehension Questions reproducible (page 46).

Just the (Fish) Facts

Read the book *Big Al*
by Andrew Clements. Answer the questions below.

Big Fish
Saves the Day

Where did this story
happen?

_____
_____
_____
_____
_____

Who was Big Al?

_____
_____
_____
_____
_____

What did Big Al do to try to make friends
with the other fish?

_____
_____
_____

Did Big Al get away from the fisherman?
How?

_____
_____
_____
_____

What did Big Al do when he saw the fish
in the net?

_____
_____
_____
_____

Question Creators

Cut apart and give one
card to each group to use with the Creating
and Answering Higher-Order Questions activity (page 42).

Cause and Effect: Write a lower-order question that requires the reader to find a cause
and/or effect from the passage. Fill in a question below or come up with your own.
• What caused_____ to_____ ?
• What was the effect of _____ ?
• What happened when_____ ?
• What might happen if_____ ?
• Why did _____ happen?

Main Events: Write a lower-order question about the events. Fill in one question below
or come up with your own.
• What happened before_____ ?
• What happened after _____ ?
• What happened in between _____ and _____ ?

Comparing and Contrasting: Write a question that requires the reader to compare
and/or contrast something from the passage. Fill in a question below or come up with
your own.
• How is_____ similar to _____ ?
• How is_____ different from_____ ?
• How are_____ and _____ similar?
• How are_____ and _____ different?

Author's Purpose: Write a higher-order question that requires the reader to think
about the author's purpose. Fill in a question below or come up with your own.
• Why did the author write_____ ?
• What did the author mean when he or she wrote_____ ?
• Why do you think the author wrote_____ ?

Character: Write a higher-order question that requires the reader to think about the
character(s). Fill in a question below or come up with your own.
• Why do you think the character _____ ?
• What do you think the character meant when he or she _____ ?
• How would you describe the character of_____ ?

First-Rate Reading™: Comprehension • CD-104015 • © Carson-Dellosa
Basics

Higher-Order Question Starters

Use the question starters to create
higher-order questions for classmates to answer. Your teacher will tell you
which questions to copy and complete.

1. Why do you think . . . ?
2. How do you think . . . ?
3. What would you do if . . . ?
4. What do you think caused . . . ?
5. What was the effect of . . . ?
6. How was . . . ?
7. If you . . . ?
8. Why do you think the author . . . ?
9. How does the author . . . ?
10. What do you think might happen if . . . ?
11. How is _____ similar to _____ . . . ?
12. How is _____ different from_____ . . . ?
13. What does _____ remind you of?
14. What do you think the author meant when he or she wrote . . . ?
15. What does the word _____ mean in the sentence "_____"?
16. What would you say is the main idea of . . . ?
17. Why . . . ?
18. What word would you use to describe the story/article/book? Why?

For narrative text only:
1. How do characters change from the beginning to the end of the story?
2. Why do you think the character . . . ?
3. How do you think the character felt when . . . ?
4. If you were _____, what would you do if . . . ?
5. What word would you use to describe the character _____ ?
6. What do you think is the most important event in . . . ?
7. What does the character mean when he or she says . . . ?
8. Why do you think the character . . . ?
9. What might have made the character . . . ?

Higher-Order Comprehension Questions

On another piece of paper,
write and answer the questions. Your teacher
will tell you which questions to complete.

1. What is the main idea of this story?
2. Describe the main characters.
3. What is the setting? (time and place)
4. What are the main events of the story?
5. What is the problem? How is it resolved?
6. Did you like the story? Why or why not? Give examples from the story.
7. What was your favorite part? Explain why.
8. What was your least favorite part? Explain why.
9. If you were the author, what would you have done differently when you wrote this story?
10. Think of three words that would describe this story. Use examples from the story to support your choices.
11. Think of three words to describe the main character. Use examples from the story to support your choices.
12. If you were the main character, what would you have done in his or her situation?
13. What lesson can you learn from this story?
14. Do any of the characters in this story remind you of characters from other books you have read? If so, who and why?
15. Do any of the characters in this story remind you of anyone you know? If so, who and why?
16. Pick an event from the reading that reminds you of something that happened to you or someone you know. What is the event, and what does it remind you of?
17. How did this story make you feel? Why?
18. If you could be any character from the story, who would you be and why?
19. Did any part of the story confuse you? If so, what part and why?
20. Did any of the characters change during the story? If so, who and how?

First-Rate Reading™: Comprehension • CD-104015 • © Carson-Dellosa
Basics

Higher-Order Scavenger Hunt

Obtain several copies of a simple book that most students can read independently. Make sure that the book you choose has answers to the questions on the Higher-Order Scavenger Hunt reproducible (page 48). Read the book aloud to students. Assign students to groups of four and give each group a copy of the book and four copies of the reproducible. Instruct students not to open the books. Review the scavenger hunt questions as a class. Explain that

students will be answering all of the questions independently, then comparing answers with the rest of the group. Let students begin writing answers to the questions. If a student has trouble finding an answer, let her consult other group members as before but explain that not all correct answers will be the same. When all questions have been answered by group members, instruct them to compare answers and keep track of how many different answers there are for each question. As a class, discuss the questions and answers, including how many different answers there are. Finally, explain that these questions are higher-order because they require students to use opinions about the author's message, as well as personal experience about the topic.

Charting the Answers

Review the two types of comprehension questions: lower-order and higher-order. By understanding the type of question being asked, students will also understand how to answer the question. Draw a two-row, three-column chart on the board. Above the left column, write *Question*. Above the middle column, write *Definition*. Above the right column, write *Answer*. Write the words *lower-order* and *higher-order* in the two spaces of the first column. (See right for an example.) Guide students through a discussion. First, define lower-order questions for students as questions with answers that can be found directly in the text. Write this definition in the middle column. Ask, "How would you find the answer to a lower-order

Question	Definition	Answer
Lower-Order	The answer can be found directly (right there) in the text.	Look in the book.
Higher-Order	The author has a few sentences about it. The reader must use this information and what he already knows to answer.	Look in the book and use your own experiences to answer the question.

question?" Students should respond that they would look in the book for the answer. Write this in the right column. Repeat with higher-order questions. At the end of the lesson, remind students that knowing the question will also help them know the answer.

Name _____

Higher-Order Scavenger Hunt

Answer the questions. Then,
compare answers with your group members.

1. What lessons did the author want this book to teach?

_____

_____

_____

2. How do you know that this is what the author meant?

_____

_____

_____

3. In your opinion, is this a good lesson to learn? Why or why not?

_____

_____

_____

4. Can you think of a time when you felt like a character in this book?
   Write about it on the lines below.

_____

_____

_____

_____

_____

_____

First-Rate Reading™: Comprehension • CD-104015 • © Carson-Dellosa
Basics

Literature Dictionary

Definitions for words can make great answers for lower-order questions. Read a book that defines words in the text, such as *The Three Little Javelinas* by Susan Lowell (Rising Moon, 1992). Tell students that this book contains words and ideas drawn from Native American, Mexican, and the US Old West cultures. Write the following words on the board: *javelina, dust storm, saguaro, ha'u, palo verde, adobe,* and *sí*. Ask, "What do each of these words mean?" If students cannot answer the question, explain that the author has defined these words in the book. Challenge students to listen closely so that they can figure out the words from the southwestern United States. Let students help future readers by writing a dictionary of words from the southwestern United States. Reread the book. At each word listed above, ask, "What does this word mean?" Give each student a piece of white paper. Have each student fold the paper in half twice, then cut along the fold lines to make four individual pages. Have each student stack the pages and staple them on the left side to create a mini-book. On the front cover, have each student write *My Southwestern Dictionary by Krystal*. Help students alphabetize the words, then have them write the first word on the backs of their cover pages. Challenge students to write a definition for each word. (Remind students that the author has written this information in the book.) Have each student either draw and color a small picture illustrating the object or write a sentence using the word since *sí* and *ha'u* are not easily illustrated. Close the lesson by saying that when a question is answered plainly in the text, it is called a lower-order question.

Characters Growing Up

Check out several books from a series in which the main character moves from one grade to the next, such as *Junie B. Jones and a Little Monkey Business* (Random House, 1993) and *Junie B., First Grader: Shipwrecked* (Random House, 2004) by Barbara Park, or *Ramona and Her Mother* (HarperCollins, 1990) and *Ramona Quimby, Age 8* (HarperCollins, 1992) by Beverly Cleary. Over a few weeks, read one chapter of the first book aloud each day. Have students review what happened to the character in previous chapters before going on to the next. Look for features that are consistent in the book. Ask, "How did the author organize the book? Is the book divided into chapters, or is it written as one long story?" Write answers on the board. Then, encourage students to think about the dialogue, theme, plot, etc., and how that author used each one to tell the story. For example, ask, "Was the book written in first person? What was the language like in the book?" Write these other features on the board. Next, read the book that takes place after the character goes to the next grade. Challenge students to find out if the author includes similar features in the new book. After each chapter, have students compare this book to the previous book. Ask, "What is the same? What is different?" Finally, ask how comparing books helped students understand the content.

Recognizing Story Structure

Introduction

Stories may differ in many ways, but most have a basic structure that is recognizable. Recognizing story structure improves students' understanding and memories of stories. Knowledge of plot elements, including characters, setting, sequence, problem, and resolution will increase comprehension. As students learn to identify specific elements in a story, they are better able to understand what they read. Also, the idea of structure can be used to introduce students to visual organizational elements, such as graphics, titles, bold type, etc.

Mapping Stories

Teach students how to create story maps to increase their understanding of story structure and improve reading comprehension. This visual organizational tool helps the reader locate and organize the elements and sequence of a story. Select a book to read to students, such as *The Relatives Came* by Cynthia Rylant (Aladdin, 1993) or *Dinosaurs Before Dark* by Mary Pope Osborne (Random House, 1992). Or, use an easier book, such as *Frog and Toad Are Friends* by Arnold Lobel (Harper Trophy, 1979) and have students read one chapter independently. Give each student a copy of the Story Map reproducible (page 51). Explain that organizing their ideas about the story will help students better understand the plot of the story. Have students use the story to complete the information on the Story Map page. This includes the main characters, setting, problem, main events, and solution. Have students complete the page independently and then compare responses in class.

Identifying Author's Craft and Text Structure

Author's craft and text structure refer to things a writer uses to help the reader understand the text, such as bold and italicized print, headings, graphics, captions, vocabulary word definitions, etc. These are most often present in nonfiction or informational text. Tell students that being able to recognize the author's craft and text structure will help them better understand what they read. Authors use different techniques to help readers understand the text. To illustrate this, give each student a copy of a passage of informational text and make a transparency of that passage for whole-group modeling. Think aloud and make notes on the transparency as you read the passage. Ask, "What do I notice about the way this passage is written? What does this heading/graphic/photo/etc., tell me about what I will read? Why does the author put this word in these dark, thick letters? This print is called bold print, and the author uses it to let us know that this word is very important. I notice that the author has titled this paragraph 'Where They Live.' This is a subheading, and it lets me know that this section will be about where manatees live." As you take notes, underline, etc., on the overhead, have students do the same on their copies. Have students work in small groups or pairs to practice identifying an author's craft and text structure with a different passage. Reconvene as a group and discuss.

Name _____

Story Map

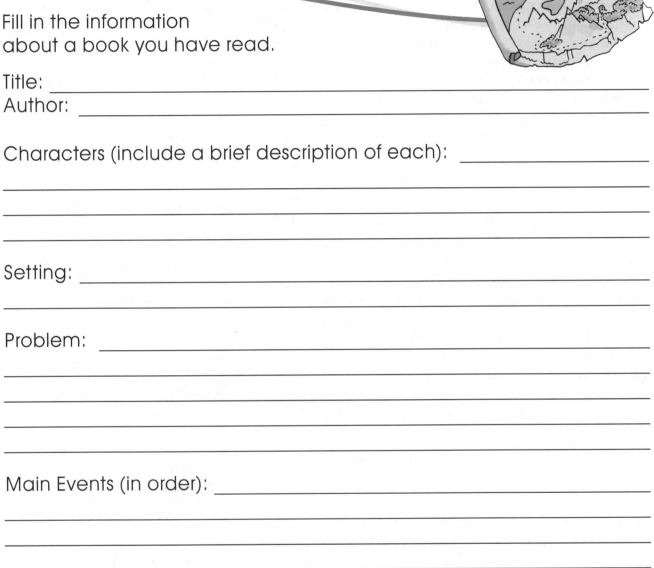

Fill in the information
about a book you have read.

Title: _____

Author: _____

Characters (include a brief description of each): _____

_____

_____

_____

Setting: _____

_____

Problem: _____

_____

_____

_____

_____

Main Events (in order): _____

_____

_____

_____

_____

_____

Solution: _____

_____

_____

Sewing Up Sequencing

Sequencing a story can help students recall details. Illustrate sequencing with a hands-on activity using *Joseph Had a Little Overcoat* by Simms Taback (Viking, 1999). Discuss the sequence of the events and list the items that Joseph made from his coat (*overcoat, jacket, vest, scarf, necktie, handkerchief, button, a story*) randomly on the board. Give each student a large piece of construction paper. Have students place the papers lengthwise and draw and color sewing needles in the upper left corners. This will be the beginning of their pictures showing the sequence of the story. Next, have students write the story sequence by referring to the words on the board. Caution students that the words are out of order. Have students start writing at the eye ends of their needles, making the words curve like thread coming out of the needles. Have students use colorful markers to write. Tell students to write about what happened in the story by repeatedly asking themselves, "What happened next?" until they reach the end of the story. Encourage students to write their sentences in curvy lines over the entire paper. Review the sequence and reread the story if necessary. Tell students that making pictures, or graphics, of the sequence helped them focus on the story.

Characters Building Structure

Help students categorize complex information from literature. Give each student a copy of the Characters Building Structure reproducible (page 53) and discuss the categories implied by each question: setting, initiating events, internal reactions, goals, attempts, and outcomes. Then, share a book, such as *Thank You, Mr. Falker* by Patricia Polacco (Philomel, 1998), and review how parts of the story can be categorized on the reproducible. Possible answers for this book are that the main *setting* is first a school in Michigan and then one in California; *initiating events* are Trisha tasting the honey and her first reading struggles; *internal reactions* are her fear of being teased and her continuing struggle to read; *goals* are Trisha's desire to read and to hide her disability and Mr. Falker's desire to help her; *attempts* could be Trisha trying to read and working with her teacher and speech therapist; and *outcomes* are that Tricia learns to read and becomes a writer. Place copies of the book at a center. Schedule time for students to reread the book and fill in the reproducible. Assess students' understanding by having them use copies of the reproducible to analyze other books.

Genre Study

Explain that literary genres are the different categories of reading material. If students can distinguish between genres, they will learn to recognize literary patterns. Literature can be divided into more complex genres than those included here, but the categories below are appropriate for second and third graders. Display the Genres reproducible (page 54) as you teach literary genres. First, explain that text can be divided into categories called *genres*. Then, review each genre and give familiar examples of each. Next, assign students to small groups. Give each group a book and have them determine the type of genre it is. Instruct groups to be prepared to support their choice of genre with evidence. For example, a group who has the book *The Cat in the Hat* by Dr. Seuss (Random House, 1957) might say, "This book is fantasy because it has a talking cat and fish, which could never really happen." Include overlapping books, such as the Scooby-Doo™ series, which are mysteries but can also be fantasy because of the talking dog. Genres answers are 1. B; 2. C; 3. F; 4. E; 5. D; 6. G; 7. A. For further practice, assign the Genre Scavenger Hunt (page 55). To assess knowledge of genres, use the Genre Quiz (page 56). Genre Quiz answers are 1. G; 2. B; 3. F; 4. E; 5. D; 6. A; 7, C.

Name _____

Characters Building Structure

Read a book
and answer the questions below.

1. What is the setting of the book? _____
_____

2. What events start the main plot of the story? _____
_____
_____

3. How do the main characters react to these events? _____
_____
_____
_____

4. What are the main characters' goals? _____
_____
_____
_____

5. How do the characters try to reach these goals? _____
_____
_____
_____

6. What happens to the main characters at the end of the story?
_____
_____
_____

Genres

Draw a line from each genre
to its correct description on the right.

1. Informational

    A. This genre can be fiction or nonfiction and contains poems.

    B. This genre is nonfiction and gives information, like a book about caring for a pet or a book about sea animals.

2. Realistic Fiction

    C. This genre is fiction that could happen. Two examples are a book about a boy who wants to be class president or a book about a girl who argues with her sister.

3. Fantasy Fiction

    D. This genre is fiction based on something that happened in history (the past). An example is a made-up story about a girl growing up during World War II.

4. Mystery

5. Historical Fiction

    E. This genre can be fiction or nonfiction and it contains a mystery to be solved.

    F. This genre is fiction that could never really happen, like a book with talking animals or about a boy who can fly.

6. Biography

    G. This genre is nonfiction and is a true story about a person's life. If it is written by the person whom the story is about, the prefix *auto-* is in front of the word.

7. Poetry

Genre Scavenger Hunt

Go on a scavenger hunt
in your school or classroom library. Use
the genre column below to find books in the library.
Write the title of each book you find and your reasons for choosing
that book in the correct columns.

Genre	Book title	Why did you pick this book?
Historical Fiction	_____	_____
	_____	_____
Poetry	_____	_____
	_____	_____
Mystery	_____	_____
	_____	_____
Realistic Fiction	_____	_____
	_____	_____
Autobiography	_____	_____
	_____	_____
Informational	_____	_____
	_____	_____
Fantasy Fiction	_____	_____
	_____	_____
Biography	_____	_____
	_____	_____

Genre Quiz

Write the letter of the
correct example on the right
beside the correct genre on the left.

Genre	Example
1. Informational	A. *Bluestem* by Frances Arrington (Philomel, 2000): a made-up story about two sisters and their experiences in the 1870s.
2. Fantasy Fiction	B. *Charlotte's Web* by E. B. White (HarperCollins, 1976): a book about a talking pig and spider who become best friends.
3. Realistic Fiction	C. *Where the Sidewalk Ends: the Poems and Drawings of Shel Silverstein* by Shel Silverstein (HarperCollins, 1974): a collection of poems and drawings.
4. Biography/ Autobiography	D. *Encyclopedia Brown: Boy Detective* by Donald Sobol (Skylark, 1985): a book about a boy who is called Encyclopedia Brown because he can solve mysteries.
5. Mystery	E. *Gutsy Girls: Young Women Who Dare* by Tina Schwager, Elizabeth Verdick, and Michele Scherger (Free Spirit, 1999): true stories about the lives of young women with unusual hobbies and careers.
6. Historical Fiction	F. *Beezus and Ramona* by Beverly Cleary (HarperCollins, 1990): a story of two sisters who do not get along.
7. Poetry	G. *Cats and Kittens* by Katherine Starke (Usborne, 1998): information about caring for cats and kittens.

First-Rate Reading™: Comprehension • CD-104015 • © Carson-Dellosa
Basics

Summarizing

Introduction

Summarizing and inferring main idea are difficult tasks for young readers because they are abstract skills. Summarizing requires readers to understand information they have read and put it into their own words. An example that can simplify this process is to compare a nonfiction book about a specific animal with a dictionary entry and an encyclopedia entry. Compare the amount of information in each and compare the type of information in the dictionary and encyclopedia entries. If students can identify a main idea and the details that are necessary to support that idea, they can summarize that information.

Inferring Detectives

Students need to learn how to infer information from text. Introduce this skill using small pieces of text in isolation in which students can focus only on inferring the meaning. Have students read the sentences and make inferences based on the text's information. Let students be reading detectives and have them find clues in the text that lead them to understand what the author has not stated directly. Provide examples, such as, "The cat curled up next to the heater to warm herself." Help students infer that it is a cold day or that the cat just came inside the house. When students make inferences, they combine prior knowledge and experience with the information given in the text. Read the following text to students. *As Annie finished packing for her trip, her mother came into her room and said, "Before you close your suitcase, make sure you packed your long underwear, heavy coat, lined boots, hat, and scarf."* Have students make inferences about the current climate found in Annie's destination or the weather forecast for that location. Use the Inferring reproducible (page 58) to have students practice this skill.

Summarization with Dramatizations

Readers' theater and other forms of dramatization are excellent activities for teaching and practicing comprehension. Although readers' theater overlaps into the area of fluency, it aids comprehension because students must comprehend the text in order to summarize it in play format or act it out as they read. Have students work in small groups to retell a story in the form of a play. Explain how to write stories in play format. Have each group write the part for one of the characters or the narrator. Select a student from each group to act out the part of the play her group has written. Give students time to practice before performing for the rest of the class. Another variation is to have each group summarize the story by rewriting it in their own words. Have each group act out their version of the story. Allow the use of student-created (or brought from home) props, set backgrounds, etc., when students dramatically summarize the story.

Inferring

Read the sentences below. Use the information to make inferences, then write them on the blanks. In the last section, write a few sentences about a topic and have a partner make an inference based on them.

Carter unwrapped the present. He tore open the box and looked inside. He opened his eyes wide, smiled brightly, and said, "Wow!"

You can infer that Carter_____ .

Our neighbors have a dog. He wags his tail when we walk by. He lets the mail carrier pet him. One time, he licked my little brother!

You can infer that the dog is _____ .

Malinda was sitting on the sidewalk wearing her skates. She was crying and holding her arm. She had a big scrape on her elbow.

You can infer that Malinda_____ .

Your information: _____

_____

_____

_____

You can infer that _____

_____

_____ .

First-Rate Reading™: Comprehension • CD-104015 • © Carson-Dellosa
Basics

Fast Writes

Fast writes can help students get started writing summaries. Immediately after reading a selection, have students quickly jot down phrases, words, or sentences that will be used as notes for summarizing the story orally. Make sure that the emphasis is on content and not on sentence structure, spelling, punctuation, etc. Have students share the words and phrases that they wrote. Or, model a fast write by summarizing a lesson taught in science or social studies. Model the completion of the Fast Write reproducible (page 60) using a short, easy fiction book, such as *Freckle Juice* by Judy Blume (Simon and Schuster, 1971). As you demonstrate how to use the fast write to give an oral summary, either summarize the story at the end of the reading or pause as you read each fact and update the reproducible. For example, for this story, some of the summary might read: *Event/Fact#1: Andrew wants freckles. Event/Fact #2: Andrew asks Nicky how to get freckles. Event/Fact #3: Sharon offers to sell her secret freckle recipe to Andrew for 50 cents.* To demonstrate with nonfiction, use the reproducible to summarize material recently taught in class. Finally, give each student a copy of the reproducible to use for summarizing his own reading.

Summarizing with Sentence Frames and Story Cards

Students are often overwhelmed when asked to summarize text. Use summary frames to help students organize events in the correct sequence and identify key elements in the story. Have students read an easy story, such as *Flat Stanley* by Jeff Brown (Harper & Row, 1964). Help students summarize the key elements of the story as you model the exercise on a transparency copy of the Sentence Frames reproducible (page 61). For example, in the first section, answers for *Flat Stanley* might be: *This story begins with Stanley being flattened by a bulletin board, continues with Stanley enjoying his flatness by having adventures, and ends with Stanley tiring of being flat and his brother Arthur making Stanley his normal size again.* Students can apply this reproducible to almost any narrative passage. Or, use the Story Summary reproducible (page 62) as an additional reference. Laminate copies of the page and let students use them with write-on/wipe-away markers if desired. First, have each student record critical story elements. Then, have her use the elements to write a paragraph summary for the story or passage on a separate sheet of paper. Similarly, have students use the Summarizing Informational Text (page 63) for nonfiction passages and articles.

Fast Write

Retell the main events or facts
on the lines below. You do not need to write
in complete sentences. Write only important words
and ideas, but write enough information to be able to retell the text.

Event/Fact #1: _____

_____

Event/Fact #2: _____

_____

Event/Fact #3: _____

_____

Event/Fact #4: _____

_____

Event/Fact #5: _____

_____

Event/Fact #6: _____

_____

Event/Fact #7: _____

_____

Event/Fact #8: _____

_____

First-Rate Reading™: Comprehension • CD-104015 • © Carson-Dellosa
Basics

Sentence Frames

Summarizing
Narrative

Use the following sentence
frames to summarize the story.

This story begins with _____,
continues with _____,
and ends with _____.

The main character in this story wanted _____

_____,

but _____

_____,

so _____

_____.

The first thing that happens in this story is _____

_____

Then, _____

_____

After that, _____

_____.

It ends when _____

_____.

This story is mainly about a _____
who _____

_____.

The main characters in this story are _____.
The problem is _____.
The solution is _____.
The title of this story is _____.
This is a good title because _____

_____.

Story Summary

Fill out the information
to summarize a story.

Stories must have **characters**: people or animals in the story. Main
characters are most important. Supporting characters help tell the story.
List the main characters in the story: _____
_____
_____

List the supporting characters in the story: _____
_____
_____

Sometimes a story has several problems, but there is always one major
problem that is usually the plot or main idea.
What is the problem in the story? _____
Which character is facing this problem? _____
Do the characters face smaller problems or only one major problem?
_____

An **event** is something that happens. The main events are the most
important things that happen in the story. When summarizing the main
events, use order words like *first, second, next, then,* etc., to help you.
List the main events in the story: _____
_____
_____

The **solution** (how the problem was solved) usually comes near the
end of the story. What is the solution in the story? _____
_____

Which character(s) helped to solve the problem and how? _____
_____

Summarizing Informational Text

Use one or more of the following
sentence frames to help you summarize the article.

This article is mainly about _____ .
It describes _____ .
I learned that _____

_____ .

The main idea of this article is _____

_____ .
Some of the details that I read about in the article are _____

_____

_____ .

This article is about _____ ,
which are _____ .
In the article, it says that _____

_____ .
I learned that _____

_____ .

In this article, I learned that _____

_____ .
Also, _____

_____

_____ .

Class Newsletter

Have students create a class newsletter to summarize events happening in the classroom and school. Give each student a piece of paper. Direct each student to draw two vertical lines on the paper to create three columns. Or, provide each student with a copy of the Newspaper Column reproducible (page 65). Explain that newsletters often have columns like a newspaper. Show a real newspaper as an example. Have students write paragraphs between the lines of the columns. Tell students that they should only write about the most important issues or events that are happening in the classroom. Have students brainstorm topics, such as upcoming tests, interesting class projects, homework assignments, and big news at the school. Write students' ideas on the board. Discuss some not-so-important topics. Ask, "Is it important to tell parents who wore striped socks today or that Jeffrey broke his pencil yesterday?" Students will answer, "No!" Reinforce the idea that students should only write about important information. Direct students to write their paragraphs. Encourage the "journalists" to add pictures and explain that using pictures is an efficient way to convey information. Remind students that being able to pick out important information will help them read. When students finish, compile the papers into a class newsletter. Allow students, class visitors, parents, etc., to read the newsletter. Repeat this activity once a month or season.

We CAN Summarize!

When students can summarize a story, they can remember the most important events. A key part of summarizing is condensing information (squeezing it down) into one or two sentences. Have students visualize an aluminum soda can. Explain that it is tall at first, but when it is empty, it can be squeezed down. It's still a soda can, but it takes up less space. As an example, find a short passage from a chapter book (no more than one paragraph), write it on the tall soda can on the We CAN Summarize reproducible (page 66) and copy the reproducible for each student. Tell students to read the information on the tall soda can on their reproducibles. Then, have students think about what is most important to the passage and direct them to write a "squeezed down" version on the shorter, crumpled can. Have students share their condensed versions. Point out that even though students have different answers, they are still correct; they just used their own words to retell the information. Have students cut out the cans on their reproducibles. Cover a bulletin board with aluminum foil to create a display for students' cans. Then, staple the taller cans in the middle and place the squished cans next to the taller cans. If desired, reuse empty soda cans by attaching them around the bulletin board with hook-and-loop tape. Title the board "We CAN Summarize!"

First-Rate Reading™: Comprehension • CD-104015 • © Carson-Dellosa
Basics

Newspaper Column

Use the boxes below to write information and draw pictures for the class newsletter. Include as many details as possible to make the information interesting for the reader.

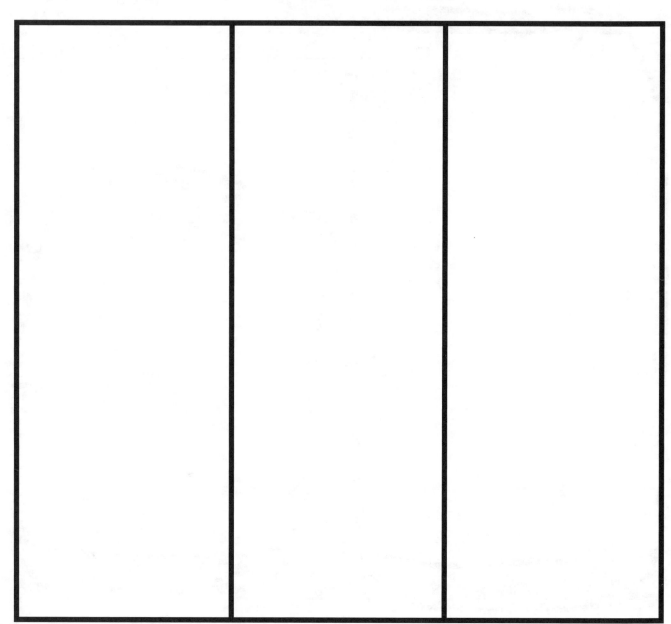

We CAN Summarize

Read the passage
on the first can. Think about what is important.
Then, write a brief summary on the second can.

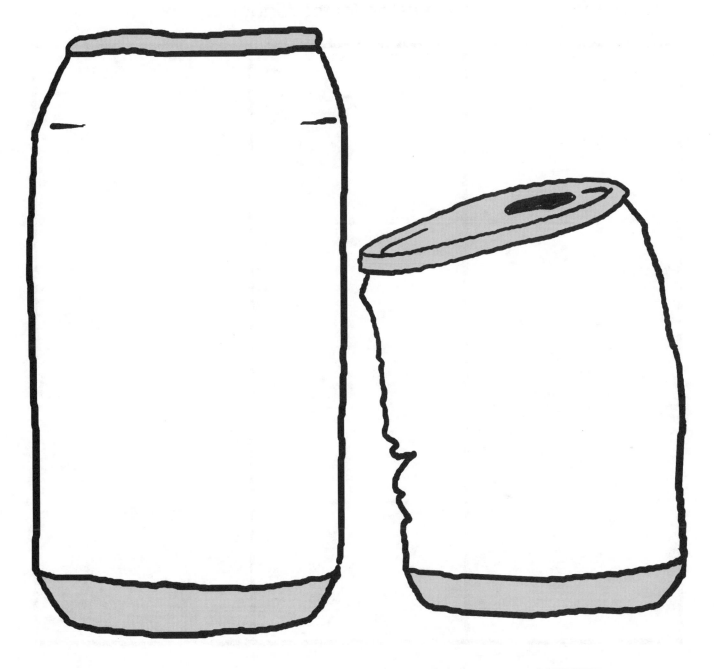

First-Rate Reading™: Comprehension • CD-104015 • © Carson-Dellosa
Basics

Outlining to Summarize

Outlining is a skill that many teachers use with older students, but younger students can also benefit from learning a simplified version of this strategy. Outlining is especially effective with informational text. Motivate students to learn the strategy by telling them that they will learn something that many high school and even college students use! Read and discuss a simple and well-structured passage. Ensure that students understand the material but focus on whether students are learning the strategy at this point, and not on whether they are comprehending the text or deciphering the main idea. On a transparency, the board, or chart paper, model the steps for creating an outline as you think aloud. Keep it simple and do not use too many subheadings. Talk through each step, referring back to the text as students follow. For example, "The passage is about snow, so I will begin my outline with the heading *Snow*. As I skim and reread parts of the article, I see that this first section of the article is about how snowflakes form. *How Snowflakes Form* is a subheading in the article, so I will begin with a number one for my outline and write the heading *How Snowflakes Form* because that is the first topic discussed. As I refer to this section of the article, I see that snowflakes are made of water; the water gathers around tiny bits of dirt, and then it freezes when wind blows it high into the atmosphere. I will summarize that in a list in my outline under the *How Snowflakes Form* heading. I will write *a. made of water, b. water forms around dirt,* and *c. freezes when wind blows high into atmosphere.*" Consider using Roman numerals if students have already learned them in math. Subcategories can be included, as well, if the article calls for them and students are ready. When you finish modeling the entire outline, have students work as a class to summarize another article in outline form on the board or on chart paper. Use this class collaboration to reteach, guide, and correct as necessary. Have students work in small groups or pairs to practice until they are able to independently summarize with outlines.

Summarizing with Newspaper Articles

Have students practice summarizing by writing newspaper articles about assigned readings. Use examples of actual newspaper articles to discuss the style of writing found in newspapers. Point out how a headline is not usually written as a complete sentence and is designed to capture readers' attention as well as state the main idea. Share articles from different sections of the paper, such as the sports and current events sections. Find examples that illustrate how reporters state facts, how they include quotes from witnesses, how photos include captions, etc. Then, as a class, summarize an article by answering the five "w" questions (*who, what, when, where,* and *why*). Demonstrate how to summarize that information into a concise paragraph. Next, have each student use the Newspaper Article reproducible (page 68) to outline and summarize an assigned informational article.

Newspaper Article

Read the article. Fill
in the blanks below to summarize the article.

Newspaper article title/headline: _____

Newspaper section: _____

By: _____

On the lines below, write the answers to the questions according to the information you read in the article.

Who?: _____

What?: _____

When?: _____

Where?: _____

Why?: _____

Write a short paragraph summarizing the article: _____

_____

_____

_____

_____

First-Rate Reading™: Comprehension • CD-104015 • © Carson-Dellosa
Basics

Book Boxes

Book boxes are a creative and fun way for students to summarize stories and books. A book box is filled with objects that symbolize the main parts, elements, themes, characters, etc., of a story. Before assigning this project for the first time, prepare a box based on a familiar story and present it to the class. For example, a book box based on *Charlotte's Web* by E. B. White (HarperCollins, 1976) might include string (to represent Charlotte's webs), small farm animal figures (to represent the characters), a photo of a barn (to represent the setting), a prize ribbon (to represent the county fair), a dictionary (to represent the spelling of the words in the webs), a friendship bracelet (to represent the theme of friendship), a baby bottle (to represent that Wilbur was a runt and Fern raised him), etc. Provide materials, such as shoe boxes, construction paper, markers, paint, string, magazine pictures, clay, cotton, etc. Have students select familiar books and create their own book boxes. Direct students to decorate their boxes using wrapping paper, paint, construction paper, etc. Have students present their book boxes to the class when complete. If all students use the same book, encourage the class to guess what each item in the boxes represents. If students complete the boxes for self-selected books or stories, have them explain each box item and what it represents. Encourage students to be creative and consider allowing them to make items if necessary, such as drawing a barn if a photo is unavailable.

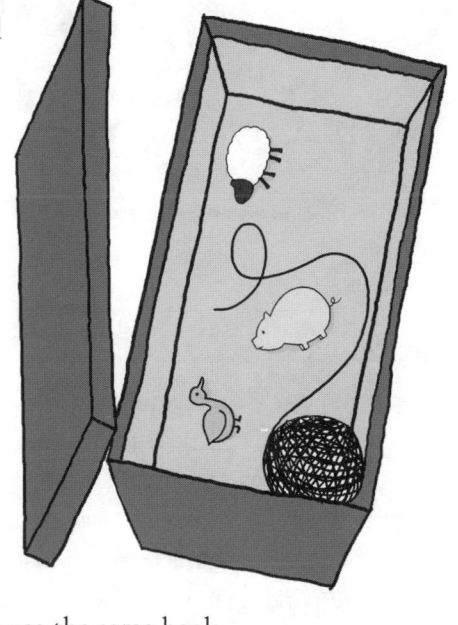

I eat eucalyptus leaves. I live in lowland eucalyptus forests in Australia. I am small and gray and furry with a black nose. I am a marsupial.

Summary Illustrations

Challenge students to summarize a passage or story by using illustrations to represent the key elements or ideas. These illustrative summaries are an excellent alternative assessment to use with struggling readers or writers who may be more successful in depicting the main ideas of the text with pictures. For example, have students read an article about a particular animal that includes its diet, physical description, habitat, etc. Then, assign students to small groups and give each group poster board or butcher paper. Have each group summarize the article. The summary might include drawings of the animal, the food it eats, a map depicting its habitats, and a hazard with an "x" drawn through it. Consider having students summarize the text orally, using their completed drawings as the springboard. Divide a long article or book and have each group summarize only one section. Have each group present their summary to the class.

Interacting with Text

Introduction

Research shows that when students make personal connections to text, they are more likely to enjoy it, understand it, and remember it. Giving students opportunities to analyze, critique, judge, and respond to text gives them emotional connections to stories. The following activities encourage students to explore concepts presented in a text and also what they bring to that text. Note that journaling and other writing form the basis for most of the activities. Writing benefits students' reading comprehension while giving them opportunities to make personal connections with the text. By responding to text in writing, students can simultaneously use information from their own lives, from the information they have read, and from their prior knowledge of the world to add meaning to reading.

Dialogue Journals

Remind students that dialogue is a conversation between two or more people. Read aloud a story that students have not heard before. After reading, have students create journal entries by filling in the blanks of the following statements: *I liked _____. I think _____. I wonder _____.* After each student gives three statements about the text, have her finish the entry with a question, such as, *What do you think will happen next?* or *Do you agree with what the character did?* Then, have each student switch journals with a partner. Have partners read each other's entries, answer their questions, and add comments if desired. Then, have students return the journals and read partners' comments and responses. For additional journal entries, students can switch with different partners each time or keep the same dialogue partners for a certain amount of time. Consider completing your own journal entry and switching with a different student each time. This will motivate students and give you an opportunity to pose key questions about the text.

Character Perspective Journals

Have students write from the perspectives of characters or objects in the text. For example, if students are reading informational text about ocean animals, have each student select one animal and write a journal entry from that animal's perspective. For fiction material, have each student select a character or assign each student a character based on the reading for that day. Instruct each student to think of writing in the journal as if she is the character keeping a diary about the events that are happening in the story. Model for students how to write a diary entry or show them an example in a book that uses a diary format, such as *Diary of a Worm* by Doreen Cronin (HarperCollins, 2003).

Reader Response Diaries

Have students respond to readings by using their journals as diaries. Explain that journals can be like diaries in which students record their thoughts, ideas, experiences, feelings, questions, opinions, etc., on the reading. Many students will have difficulty with this type of journal at first because it is so unstructured. Assign a prompt to students, such as *My favorite part was . . .* or *I know how the character felt when* _____ *because . . . .* As students become more comfortable with writing responses to materials they read, provide copies of the Readers' Response Diaries reproducible (page 72) for each student, or enlarge and post it for reference. Have students use one or more of the prompts from the list when they do not know how to begin writing. Make sure students know ahead of time that they will be sharing their diary entries. After students respond to the reading, have them share their responses with partners, small groups, or the class. Complete your own entry whenever students do so and share yours, as well.

Learning Journals

Learning journal entries are an effective and simple way for students to interact with informational text. They also help you monitor student comprehension. Use these entries to initiate a class or small group discussion on the reading material. These entries do not need to be written in complete paragraphs. Instruct students to list what they learned in the reading, write down other questions they have on the topic, and list anything about the reading that they found confusing. Students can also write about the most important things they learned from the reading. Consider collecting these journals, writing comments to students, and grading the lists of what they learned to assess comprehension and guide future lessons about the topic. For example, after a reading lesson about tigers, have each student list three things he learned, such as *I learned that tigers are the largest species of the cat family. The Siberian tiger may be more than 10 feet long, including the tail. Tigers are poor climbers but are good swimmers.* Have each student designate a fourth piece of information as the most important thing he learned from the reading, such as *The most important fact I learned is that tigers are endangered.*

Readers' Response Diaries

Use one or more of the
following prompts to help you get started in your
journal. Write a prompt, then finish it in a journal entry.

- I felt . . .
- This reminded me of . . .
- I know how the character felt when _____ because . . .
- I do not understand . . .
- A question I have is . . .
- I wonder . . .
- I noticed . . .
- If I were the author, . . .
- If I were the character _____ , . . .
- I liked the part when . . .
- I disliked the part when . . .
- My favorite part was . . .
- My least favorite part was . . .
- I think . . .
- I like how the author . . .
- I do not like how the author . . .

A Look Inside

Have students interact with text by identifying a character's actions, feelings, emotions, or motives. Use the A Look Inside reproducible (page 74) to have students examine a character in a story. Copy the reproducible onto a transparency and complete it with students as an example of the activity. Then, assign the class a familiar character to use to complete the reproducibles. Encourage students to use illustrations, words, phrases, or a combination to record what they think is in the character's mind. For example, if they could see inside the mind of Martha, the dog in *Martha Speaks* by Susan Meddaugh (Houghton Mifflin, 1992), they might see the words and phrases *Isn't it time for my dinner? I dreamed I was chasing a giant meatloaf*, or even *Shut up*. They might see illustrations of alphabet soup, Helen and the family, or burglars. Allow students to refer to the text when completing this activity. Consider having students work in groups or pairs, then have them present the depictions to the class.

How Did I Change?

A sophisticated journal entry topic may not be suitable for all readers, but even on a basic level, students are capable of thinking about how knowledge changes them. Discuss a recently finished book and talk about how students are different after reading it for the first time. Perhaps they feel differently about points of view they previously held or learned some new facts. Or, maybe they just decided they like the way the author writes and want to read more books by the same author. Ask each student to choose a book that made him feel or think something different after reading it. Thoughts and feelings can be as simple as *I didn't know until reading the article that parts of the world are being repopulated with wolves* from a nonfiction text, or as insightful as *Since I read this book, I wish I had spent more time with my grandmother before she moved.* Let students explore their feelings about reading and the effects it has on them by writing in journals. Tell students that for each entry, they may decide whether to share their thoughts by letting you or other students read their entries. Assign students to small groups to encourage the sharing of entries and thoughts.

A Look Inside

Draw a character in the first
box. In the second box, write and draw
what you think you would see if you could look inside
the character's mind. Use words, phrases, and drawings.

First-Rate Reading™: Comprehension • CD-104015 • © Carson-Dellosa
Basics

Literature Reviews

Let students use the Book Reviews reproducible (page 76) to write reviews about books they have read. Prior to assigning the activity, bring in real book reviews from magazines or on-line sites. Discuss what words and phrases the reviewers use and the various topics they address. Demonstrate and review how to summarize a book using a familiar story, such as *Dinosaurs Before Dark* by Mary Pope Osborne (Random House, 1992). Elicit details about the book from students and write them on the board. As a class, decide which details are most important and include them in a class summary. For example, this book's summary could be: *Jack and Annie find a tree house full of books. They open a book about dinosaurs and go back in time. They see all kinds of dinosaurs and are in some danger but are magically able to return safely home.* Next, be sure students know the difference between summarizing and reviewing. Explain that to review books they must talk about and share their opinions about whether the books are good selections. Have students select their own books to read or reread. Encourage students to be honest and to provide support for their opinions. Have each student submit a rough draft of her review to ensure that she comprehends the story and can relate the story structure and main idea. Then, have students publish their reviews. Post the completed reviews in the school or classroom library, or compile them in a "Literature Review" class magazine.

Book Advertisements

Motivate students to interact with their favorite books by creating advertisements to sell them. Have students look through magazines to study actual ads or bring in posters advertising books. (Ask your media specialist or a local bookstore owner to donate posters that advertise familiar children's books.) Complete a simple ad with students to demonstrate this process. Read a book aloud and model writing a short summary of the book. Have students choose the most important details from the summary to include on a sample advertisement for that book. Include the title, author, illustrator, and publisher. Add an illustration or photograph that will generate interest in the book. Then, instruct students to choose books to carefully read or reread. Next, have each student write a short summary of his book to refer to while designing his ad. Tell students that their ads must be accurate and must also make viewers want to buy and read the books. Then, on pieces of poster board or large pieces of construction paper, have students write and illustrate their advertisements. Instruct each student to include his book's title, author, illustrator, and publisher. Students' ads must also include photos or illustrations, and enough information from the book to give the viewers clues about the book. Remind students to include only the most important or most interesting details in their ads. Encourage students to come up with slogans, catchy phrases, etc., to include in their advertisements. Allow students to present their ads, then post them in the reading center or combine them into a class book. Have students refer to the posters when they need information about the books.

Book Reviews

Use the space below to write
a book review. Include details from the book
to support your opinions. Add drawings around
the edges of the review.

Book Title: _____

Author: _____

Review: _____

_____

_____

_____

_____

_____

_____

_____

_____

_____

First-Rate Reading™: Comprehension • CD-104015 • © Carson-Dellosa
Basics

Sequels and New Endings

Have students continue their favorite stories by writing sequels or have them rewrite the endings. First, discuss how sometimes students do not want a story to stop, and other times, they wish things had happened differently. Have each student choose a book to continue or to rewrite its ending. After students read the books, encourage them to think about what might happen next or what might have happened in the end instead. Suggest that they have characters go on other adventures or that things be changed from the books' endings to make them more like endings students would like. Tell students to be creative but to be true to the characters and the original story lines. Instruct students to write their sequels or new endings. Then, have a class sharing day for each sequel or new ending. Each day, select a book for which students have written sequels or new endings. Read the book aloud and have students who have written sequels or new endings for that book share them with the class. Let the class ask the students questions about what events and characters they included in their sequels or new endings. If time permits, let each student turn her sequel or new ending into a book, complete with illustrations. Place student-made books in the reading center with their original counterparts.

Book Awards

Assess reading comprehension by having students read and nominate favorite books for specific book awards. Discuss the Newbery and Caldecott Medals. Explain that each year, one book receives the Newbery Medal for excellent writing in children's books, and one book receives the Caldecott Medal for excellent illustrating in children's books. If possible, allow students to research past Newbery and Caldecott winners on the Internet. Then, provide some of these books for students to review. Have students nominate their favorite books for a special book award using the Book Awards reproducible (page 78). Allow students to read the book nominees prior to selecting the class favorites, or read the book nominees aloud to the class. Conduct a vote to select the top three award winners. Another option is to come up with several awards, such as Funniest Book, Most Unique Illustrations, Wonderful Word Choice, etc. Then, have students create awards and nominate books they feel deserve these awards. Post the awards on a bulletin board or in the reading center to stimulate interest in the books.

Book Awards

Fill out this sheet to nominate
a book you think deserves an award from your class.

Award: _____

Book title: _____

Author: _____

Illustrator: _____

Reason for Nomination: _____

_____

_____

_____

_____

_____

_____

_____

First-Rate Reading™: Comprehension • CD-104015 • © Carson-Dellosa
Basics

Author Communication

Many authors and publishers have contact information listed on Web sites. Have students write letters to an author about their opinions of and reactions to reading the author's work. First, research authors who accept and respond to children's letters. Then, have students write letters asking questions or sharing how the author's writing affected them. Mail the letters to the author. Include a brief cover letter explaining the project and highlighting some of the students' questions. If mailing the letters is not an option, share the letters or display them on a bulletin board titled "Letters to the Author." If the author writes back (and many will!), have an author celebration day by sharing a book by the author, reading the author's response aloud, and posting it on a bulletin board.

Character Communication

Integrate a fun activity requiring students to really think about characters and story lines. Pique students' interest by reading a book with a really strong, perhaps slightly annoying or otherwise challenging character. Pause while reading the book aloud and ask, "Don't you wish you could just tell this character something?" As students share what they would like to say, explain that they can share those feelings in letters. Read aloud a letter of your own to the character, then finish reading the book. The next day, share a letter "written" back to you from the character. Next, let each student choose a book and write a letter to a character. Instruct students to give advice, ask the characters questions, or simply respond to the characters' behaviors and problems in the stories. After completing the first letter, have each student write a response letter from her character's perspective. Or, have each pair of students read one book. Let pairs exchange and answer letters from two different characters' perspectives. For example, one student should write to the main character, and the second student should respond from that character's perspective. The second student should write his first letter to a secondary character, and the first student should respond from the secondary character's perspective. Have students share their letters with the class.

Community Connections

Lend a sense of realism and immediacy to nonfiction reading. After students read informational text, have them write letters to appropriate officials asking questions, giving suggestions, sharing opinions, etc. For example, after reading about protecting woodland areas, have students write to local officials about what they have learned and their concerns about trees. Students can also bring in information about current events and write letters to local or state officials about causes that are important to them. If possible, do not assign topics for this project, but let them arise naturally from class reading and discussion. Students will feel more of a connection to this assignment if they can choose topics that are important to them.

Gallery of Characters

Especially as students read books with fewer pictures, their minds will fill in the visual gaps left by illustrators with their own ideas about how characters look. As each student reads a chapter book, have him jot down clues the author gives about what a character looks like. Remind students that the author may describe the character's appearance (hair and eye color, etc.) but that other traits can also affect how the portrait should look. For example, if a character is described as sad, then ask students if they would be likely to draw the character with a big smile on his face. Have each student choose a favorite book and draw a character portrait that represents a character's personality, feelings, problems, etc. Explain that when students are finished with the portrait, a person who has never read the story should be able to look at it and know what the character is like. Instruct students not to label or share their drawings or the identities of the characters. Then, post all of the unlabeled portraits on a bulletin board and gather the books students used. Work with each student to find a few sentences describing the character he chose. Then, read relevant passages from the book and allow other students to guess which character portrait matches the passage.

Summary through Visual Medium

This activity can involve the whole class and even the entire school if other teachers participate. Complete the activity before an open house or parents' night to show off students' work. Encourage students to think about books that many students have read and enjoyed and that are meaningful to them. Suggest titles or have students propose their favorites. List all suggestions on the board. Then, assign students to the following roles: creating ballots, distributing ballots, tallying votes, brainstorming a good illustration scene, illustrating and coloring the drawing, adding text to the drawing, posting the drawing, and creating the summary and text to go with the drawing. Explain all of these roles as the project progresses. Have assigned students create and distribute ballots. When voting is complete, collect the ballots and have students tally the votes. Arrange for a run-off if necessary. Next, let the brainstormers suggest a scene from the book to illustrate. Student artists should then illustrate the scene on a sheet of bulletin board paper cut to fit the outside door of the classroom. The students creating the summary should first copy the text from the illustrated scene, then write a brief summary of the book, listing the author, original illustrator (if there is one), and publication information. Post the illustration and summary on the outside of the door. (Laminate the drawing and summary if the classroom door is exposed to weather.) Other teachers may also choose to reinforce literature by completing this activity. If other classes participate, coordinate a date for the door gallery "premiere." On gallery day, take the class on a tour. Did any other class choose the same book or even the same scene? Pause at several doors to read the summaries and introduce students to other texts.